ROSANNA KELLY is a translat
is the eldest of the three children
Linda & Laurence Kelly. She li
husband, the novelist and journ........ ...., ...,
and with her son Alexander Reviakin.

LINDA

A Writer's Journey

edited & illustrated by

Rosanna Kelly

First edition, limited to 100 copies

©2020 Rosanna Kelly
ISBN 0-936315-47-4
STARHAVEN, 42 Frognal, London NW3 6AG
books@starhaven.org.uk

Typeset in Garamond

Contents:

Photograph of Linda in 1991
taken by Nicholas Kelly

Preface

Linda's memorial service at the Roman Catholic Church of St Mary's of the Angels in January 2019 was a joyous occasion. Among the celebrations of her life was a wonderful piece of solo singing by her grandson, and her brother-in-law, the writer Thomas Pakenham, delivered the address. She was a woman to celebrate privately and publicly. She was, for me, the leading historical writer of her generation. In the unfair way of life, she was also the best possible company, very beautiful and in possession of two of life's greatest attributes: courage and a merciful heart. Whether as a member of the congregation you were a believer, or whether you put scientific materialism above metaphysics, the same sense of the miraculous pervaded. Believers know that their Creator celebrates all life and knows of the death of a sparrow. As modern scientists like Stephen Hawking delve deeper and deeper into the chemical and physical uniqueness of creation, they too become infected with a sense of the miraculous. And a sense, too, of life's darker sides: its vulnerability to accident and corruption.

An historical writer is different from an historian or an historical novelist. Historians correlate discoveries old and new to assemble a portrait of an individual or an age. Historical novelists make verbal or actual movies from such research. An historical *writer* aims to give the reader a sense of what T.S. Eliot, in his famous essay *Tradition and the Individual Talent,* called 'the present moment of the past'. Linda was extraordinarily successful at bringing her chosen times, places and people to life. Doing so does not exempt the historical writer from research or from exercising an historical imagination. Both are needed but it is a sense of court, time, person and place that determines success or failure.

Linda's arena was the mid-18th to the mid-19th century. She chose this instinctively because as a young woman she loved the Romantic poets. But the more she burrowed into the period the more she found in it correspondences and influences on her own time. The Romantic poets were writing at a time when the Industrial Revolution in Britain was changing not only Britain but the world. And changing it for both good and ill. And Linda's lively interest in people and places meant that the politics of the time were a foretaste in some respects of the London-centric politics of our own day. Marx's championing of humanity in the mass lay ahead still. Linda's subject was the fierce rivalry and competition inhabiting a world of privileged elites.

Her masterpiece, in my view, is her study of the Whig Party centred at Holland House and dominated by a nephew of Charles James Fox, Lord Holland and his wife. For much of the time the Whigs were out of office as the nation, perhaps wisely, entrusted William Pitt and the Tories with conduct of the Napoleonic War. The liberal Whigs were instinctive admirers of Napoleon and we have to remember that before he enraged Beethoven into tearing up the dedication to his Eroica Symphony, by crowning himself Emperor, Napoleon was rightly considered a rational and liberalising destroyer of repressive *ancien* regimes. But in spite of being out of power the Whigs remained always in fashion. Parties at Holland House were the best in London; indeed, famous all over Europe. When Queen Victoria ascended the throne in 1837, she longed to meet Lady Holland but could not do so as Lady Holland had divorced her husband to marry Lord Holland. Queen Victoria had a legendary crush on her first Prime Minister, the Whig Lord Melbourne. She dreaded the return of the Hollands' from tours on the Continent because she knew Lord M. would sneak off very regularly to dine at Holland House and she refused to blame him for doing so.

Linda's last historical book was a study of Talleyrand's last job, French ambassador in London. The maker of the post Napoleonic world, the restorer of intensely Tory old regimes, was the life and soul of parties held there and Linda's earlier interests in the Romantic poets found a natural home there as the Irish poet, Tom Moore, was a regular and Byron a brooding, beautiful and always alarming frequent visitor. There were lashings of sex and barely concealed scandal which the tolerant but conjugal Hollands' were well aware of but determined to ignore.

Re-reading Linda's studies I can quite understand why her generation and mine whose liberal hopes and youth were raised by the Kennedys', found this not un-dodgy family so appealing in our youth. They were natural Whigs; very rich, very privileged but tolerant as, given their private lives, they had to be. J.F.K.'s favourite book was David Cecil's *Lord M.* – a study of Melbourne.

Laurence and Linda Kelly lived for over fifty years in what felt like a large country house on the crest of Ladbroke Grove where they raised three remarkable children. To all their visitors Linda's generosity and grace and Laurence's shrewd wit mirrored the atmosphere Linda described so well in Holland House.

Grey Gowrie

Introduction

A wind is blowing off the sea and my sister, brother and I, and our two cousins, Maria and Eliza, are sitting in a clump of spikey New Zealand flax under the shelter of a stone wall, listening spellbound to my mother's voice as she reads us the *Adventures of Brigadier Gerard*. The story of how he slew the fox (by overtaking the hounds) fills us with delicious horror – our grandfather was a Master of Fox Hounds. We were staying with my half-French, half-Belgian grandmother at her seaside cottage in Ireland and our camp in the New Zealand flax was as much a retreat from her immediate domain as it was from the wind. Books were my mother's refuge all through her life – she always carried one in her handbag and quoted from Montesquieu: 'There is never any distress that an hour's reading will not relieve.'

In this book of scenes from my mother's books and of tributes to her, her love of reading emerges as a constant theme and also as a natural companion to the other great constant in her life – writing – 'the solitary occupation', notes David Pryce-Jones, 'that she obviously believed has supreme value'. But writing was something she seldom talked about at home or with friends; nor did she discuss the reviews and letters she received. The one exception I can remember was a letter she had received from Graham Greene: 'I have been reading with delight *The Young Romantics*. I admire it for its brevity and the narrative skill which keeps so many characters moving on their parallel or intersecting lives year by year.' Only after she had died, going through her papers, did we discover tributes she had received from other famous writers – Rebecca West, Paul Scott, John Wain, Claire Tomalin, Jane Ridley to name but a few. Since my mother was extraordinarily modest about her literary achievements during her life-time, the aim of this book is to give her a recognition she deserves. The title is chosen in echo of a book she created about her great friend, Alyson Spooner, *Alyson: A Painter's Journey*, though Marina Camrose suggested a tempting alternative *Les Très Riches Heures de Linda Kelly*.

The contents will, we hope, show not only what a wonderful writer my mother was but what a wonderful human being. She was, writes Pamela Woof, 'a presence that brought an air of light and peacefulness to conversations that could have sharp and prickly edges'. Regarding the reminiscences that make up the second part of this equation, I hope that my mother would have enjoyed the wit and affection they all display and which is apparent in her own memoir of her early years, that leads off the group. Regarding the section on literary appreciation, we see that the range of her writing skills and her mastery of French, English and Irish history became for many readers cumulative. Reviewing her last book, Stoddard Martin observed: 'If her ten books were to be taken as one, she would be seen as the author of a vast, engaging epic on English and French cultures and their interaction during the seventy years of massive change, 1770-1840.' This has been the inspiration for the opening part of the book, in which I have arranged selections from her work to form an overview of the drama of the Romantic period. In this my mother's deep knowledge of poetry and literature comes to the rescue often.

Poetry runs like a leitmotif through the extracts. It was part of my mother's upbringing to learn poetry: her father had written gentle and romantic Georgian poems at Oxford in the 1920s and was known by John Betjeman as 'the poet of St John's'; and her mother often read her and her siblings ballads and long narrative poems. According to her sister Valerie, 'We all had to recite a poem in order to earn our Christmas presents from our grandmother. We learnt very long ones, like Macaulay's lays, but after a while – there were numerous grandchildren – my grandmother requested shorter poems. Our cousin Philip recited a slightly dodgy limerick and was severely reproved.' My mother always had a vast store of poetry in her head and believed poetry could act as a cure for depression or keep you sane if you ever found yourself in prison.

But my mother wore her erudition lightly. As her friends record, her tastes in reading covered everything from tomes on European history to detective stories. Besides writing history, she edited a series of anthologies and helped to unearth forgotten 19th and early 20th century novels for republication. The other themes to emerge from this collection of tableaux and tributes are the joy of lunches with friends, the importance of keeping a smiling face when things are going against you, and being part of 'the mighty sum of human striving'.

Rosanna Kelly

I. Scenes from the Romantic Age

The curtain lifts on a scene from her first book, *Chatterton, The Marvellous Boy* – the young poet reading in a graveyard. It drops on a scene from her ninth book *Holland House: A History of London's Most Celebrated Salon* – the arrival of a rising star, Charles Dickens, at the dawn of a new literary age. The seven decades between are equivalent to the lifetime of some of the recurring characters: Talleyrand and Lord and Lady Holland, for example, lived through the entire Romantic era. We catch glimpses of Talleyrand from his presence at Madame de Staël's salon in pre-revolutionary France to his exile in Juniper Hall in Surrey to his arrival as the French ambassador in London in the 1830s. We see the Hollands falling in love in Italy in 1794, entertaining Byron and Sheridan to their London salon in 1812 and welcoming Talleyrand during his 1830s mission. Other characters in the cast are directly caught up in the dramas of this period of massive change: Madame Roland, sent to the guillotine at the height of the Terror; Sheridan pressing for fairer treatment of Ireland and Catholic emancipation; Victor Hugo espousing liberty with his battle cry of 'nature and truth' in the arts.

Many of the extracts are chosen for the vividness of their sense of place. London is a recurring presence, and there are memorable descriptions of the 18th century city in its theatrical, literary, musical and political guises, from Drury Lane on the first night of *School for Scandal* to Leicester Square at the time of the Gordon Riots to St James' where the poet and banker Samuel Rogers hosted his famous breakfasts. Like Samuel Johnson, my mother thought one could never tire of London. She especially loved it in the autumn when it took on the mood of an Atkinson Grimshaw painting.

The opening of Chatterton, *set in 1768, foreshadows the young poet's despairing death in a garret two years later, which would help to start the Romantic movement. The illustration is based on an 18th century print depicting the Chatterton monument.*

The church of Saint Mary Redcliffe, Bristol, had been described by Queen Elizabeth I as 'the fairest, goodliest and most famous parish church in England'. Its Gothic minster dominated Redcliffe Hill, where the Chatterton family had its lodgings. For Chatterton, born within the sound of its bells, it was a familiar place from earliest childhood. He would wander for hours in its shadowy interior, studying the medieval tombs and effigies, the intricate stone carvings, the heraldic bearings in the stained-glass windows. As a schoolboy he attended evensong there daily, the vaulted roof dim in the candlelight, choir and organ deepening the sense of Gothic mystery. On summer days he would read in the graveyard, propped up against a tomb; and sometimes he would stretch himself out in the meadows nearby and 'fix his eyes upon the church and seem as if he were in a kind of trance or ecstasy'. It was a passion which would find its deepest expression in his poetry.

On 17 April 1770 Chatterton bade farewell to Bristol and set off to try his luck in London with some 5 pounds raised by his friends to sustain him and a bundle of unpublished poems in his bag.

There is no authentic likeness of Chatterton. But we may picture him from contemporary descriptions as he set off: slight, fair-haired, rather slovenly in his dress, with large grey eyes which seemed to flash fire in anger or enthusiasm. His conversation, 'some infidelity excepted, was most captivating'; for all his sullen-ness he seems to have had great magnetism.

On his arrival in London he quickly made the rounds of the principal London editors... 'Great encouragement from them; all approved of my design; shall soon be settled,' he wrote to his mother.

He lodged first with a cousin, Mrs Ballance, at the house of Mr Walmsley, a plasterer, in Shoreditch. From the other inhabitants Herbert Croft, enquiring ten years later, was able to obtain first-hand recollections. Mr Walmsley's nephew, with whom Chatterton shared a room, said that 'not withstanding his pride and haughtiness, it was impossible to help liking him – that he lived chiefly upon a bit of bread, or a tart and some water; but he once or twice took a sheep's tongue out of his pocket'. He used to sit up almost all night, reading and writing 'for to be sure he was a spirit and never slept'...

Mrs Ballance described him as: 'Proud as Lucifer.' He

very soon quarrelled with her for calling him 'cousin Tommy' and asked if she had ever heard of a poet being called Tommy; but she assured him she knew nothing of poets and only wished he would not set up for a gentleman. Upon her recommending it to him to get into some office he stormed about the room like a madman and said he hoped with the blessing of God, very soon to be sent a prisoner to the Tower, which would make his fortune.

*

In the introduction to her sixth book, Richard Brinsley Sheridan, *Linda quotes Freya Stark's observation that* The School for Scandal *'has that sort of gaiety and charity which sweetens English literature from Chaucer, Spenser, Shakespeare, Milton, right through, an innate decency.' These same qualities, Linda argued, ran through the story of Sheridan's life. Here she describes his first great moment of success, after which he was launched as a playwright into the 'little great world' of 18th century society.*

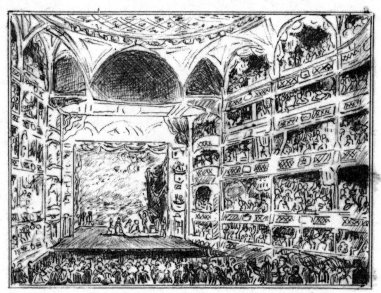

The first night of *The School for Scandal*, on 8 May 1777, was one of the great dates in theatrical history. Eagerly anticipated, it was attended by all the luminaries of the fashionable world, Mrs Crewe and the Duchess of Devonshire conspicuous amongst them. Garrick, who had superintended the rehearsals and written the prologue, was observed applauding in the highest spirits at his successor's triumph. The curtain went up at six o'clock; some time later the playwright Frederick Reynolds, who was passing outside the theatre, heard such a roar from within that, thinking the building was collapsing, he took to his heels and ran. It was the shout of applause that greeted the falling of the screen in the fourth act. So great was Sheridan's elation at his success, he told Byron years later, that 'he was knocked down and put in the watch-house for making a row in the streets and for being found intoxicated by the watchman'.

*

In 1778 Sheridan became involved with the music business when he bought a half share in the King's Theatre, Haymarket, London's main opera house at the time. This would be the venue for a series of operas sung by the great Italian castrato Gasparo Pacchierotti, who came to London for a triumphant season the next year. Among his admirers was the sensitive and musical Susanna Burney, sister of the novelist Fanny Burney. Susanna's unspoken romance with Pacchierotti, a metaphor for so many of our affections that are felt but for one reason or another never acted upon, was the subject of my mother's seventh book Susanna, the Captain & the Castrato. *The following extract introduces us to Susanna and to her father Dr Charles Burney, whose musical salon attracted a brilliant and varied company.*

Dr Burney's social position was peculiar. He made his living as a music teacher, and, in the words of Macaulay, 'belonged in fortune and station to the middle class'. Yet few nobles in the grandest mansions in St James's Street or Grosvenor Square could assemble around them so brilliant and varied a company as was sometimes to be found in Dr Burney's modest dwelling in St Martin's Street. He himself was the most delightful of companions. 'I love Burney. My heart goes out to him,' said Dr Johnson, and Johnson was only one of the lions that gathered in his drawing room.

Accustomed since childhood to her father's lively circle, with its mix of grandees, writers and performing artists, Susanna Burney's social experience was far wider than that of most well brought-up young women of the day. She was twenty-four when she wrote her letter-journals, two years younger and to judge from her portrait miniature, much prettier than her sister: bright eyed, with delicate features and a mouth just curving into a smile. Much loved by her family, she had a sweetness of disposition that showed itself from an early age. There is a characteristic story of her visiting the theatre when she was very young. The play was *Jane Shore*, and when the supposedly starving heroine paced the stage, declaring that she had not eaten for three days, it was too much for the little girl. 'Then ma'am,' she declared, 'please to accept of my orange', handing it to her from the stage box.

Susanna's letter journals give a fascinating glimpse into the operatic life of late eighteenth century London, but also her unfolding relationship with Pacchierotti – and his exasperation with Sheridan. Here Susanna records one of their long delightful conversations.

They talked of Sacchini's opera, Pacchierotti complaining

that he made him sing 'like a grasshopper', and of his latest problems with the proprietor.

'Mr Sheridan he use me very ill' he said, 'I assure you I have a great will...*come si dice* – a great mind to call him Rascal. He provoke me too much! Last night at the Opera House, he told me he wanted very much to speak to me, & beg'd of me to call on him at 12 today – At twelve accordingly, & I was very exact, I called on him – he was not at home but the servant said me however that he was sorry to disappoint me, but wd. call on me certainly between 4 & 9 this evening...'

'Have you seen him then?' asked Susanna.

'*Me?* No...Indeed he seem to behave so for the purpose to affront me – I will write him a note.'

And taking a paper from his pocket, Pacchierotti proceeded to write the following lines:

'Pacchierotti sends his Comps. to Mr Sheridan, & is very displeased to be oblig'd to call him a Rascal, but his conduct is in everything so irregular he can give no better title to so great a Breaker of his word, wch. I wish it may bring him to the gallows.'

He then drew a picture of a gallows, with a man hanging from it and himself at the bottom pulling his legs.

'Did you ever hear the like!' asked Susanna. 'You will be shocked – but had you been of the party you must have laugh'd – & Pacchierotti vowed he wd. send it tomorrow by wch. he at last half frightened me – however he ended by saying that he was not capable to send anybody such an Insult, & when they met shd. perhaps scarce reproach him for his breach of word.'

The Burneys' house was in St Martin's Street, an area of small shops and industries off Leicester Fields, now Leicester Square. Formerly owned by Sir Isaac Newton, it boasted of Newton's old observatory, a glass-sided turret at the top of the building with widespreading views over London. It was from here that Susanna witnessed one of London's most anarchic episodes.

On Friday June 2, 1780, a vast crowd of Londoners marched in procession to the Houses of Parliament. Sporting blue cockades and shouting anti-papist slogans, they were presenting a 'protestant petition' to Parliament against the supposed extension of Roman Catholic influence. Two years earlier a Roman Catholic Relief Bill, allowing a few minor concessions to Catholics while leaving them still largely excluded from public life, had passed through both Houses of Parliament without a division. It was an innocuous measure, chiefly designed to provide extra manpower by making it possible for Catholic recruits to join the army without foreswearing their religion. But it had aroused a storm of protest among extremist Protestants in England and Scotland, whose spokesman, a crackpot young aristocrat called Lord George Gordon, was now leading the procession.

As evening fell, the crowd was joined by rougher elements more interested in plundering and burning than in joining the shouts of 'No Popery'. After vainly attempting to break down the doors of the House of Commons, where they were routed by a troop of Horse Guards, the rioters surged eastwards towards Lincolns Inn Fields where they burned down the chapel of the Sardinian Embassy, then proceeded to the Bavarian Embassy, whose chapel suffered the same fate. For the moment it seemed that they were sated. On Saturday and most of Sunday there were no further disturbances, but on Sunday evening the rioting began again with far greater violence. This time Catholic property was targeted; a Catholic chapel at Moorfields was burned down and the houses of several Catholics nearby were looted. The magistrates, fearful of reprisals, were reluctant to intervene. Troops were called in, but since they were forbidden by law to fire till a magistrate had read the Riot Act, and the magistrates were usually nowhere to be found, the rioters soon learned to disregard them.

By Monday June 5th London was in a state of anarchy. A stone's throw from Leicester Fields, the Burneys' house was in the thick of some of the worst disturbances. Susanna, watching from the observatory, or gleaning the latest news from visitors, was able to give her sister a detailed description of the riots... 'Ah, my dear Fanny!' she wrote, 'How frightened & how miserable you must have been had you known what has been passing in St Martin's Street & indeed in almost every street in London.' That afternoon she had been sitting alone in the parlour, while her parents and Charlotte were out at a party nearby, when William, the manservant, came in with a face of alarm. He told her that there was terrible rioting in the streets and that a mob were breaking windows in Queen's street nearby and threatening to set fire to some of the houses because they were inhabited by Roman Catholics.

'We were soon to have some of this horrid work before own eyes,' she wrote, 'for very shortly after my father &c. returned home, & I was regretting having missed a delightful party... we heard violent shouts & huzzas from Leicester Fields & William who went to see what was the matter return'd to tell us the populace had broken into Sir Geo: Savile's house [Savile had sponsored the Catholic Relief Bill] & were then emptying it of its Furniture which having piled up in the midst of the Square, they forced Sir George's servant to bring them a candle to set fire to it – They would doubtless have set the House itself on fire had not the Horse & Foot guards prevented them

– since this time the House has been full of soldiers, to prevent it from being pulled to the Ground, wch. the Rioters have since attempted to do – the windows & even window Frames are however almost demolished, & it cuts a terrible figure. I was terrified & shocked extremely at the rage and *licence éffrenée* of the Mob–& all the horrors wch. followed this Evening's work were anticipated by my fears wch. proved to be but too well grounded – In our observatory the flames from Savile House illuminated the whole Square – & my knees were *knicky knocky* like the Frenchman's in Harlequin's Invasion... – about two in the morning all seemed quiet again & we went to bed.

*

The next three excerpts are taken from Linda's third book, a dual biography of Sarah Siddons and her brother John Kemble, who both reigned supreme on the stage between 1782 and 1817. Theatre going in the late 18th and early 19th century could be a perilous business for both the performers and the play-goers.

Mrs Siddons played eighty times, in seven different parts, in her first season, though the strain of such continued exertion was so great that she frequently fainted at the end of a performance. This was nothing to the effect on her audiences; faintings and hysterics among the sensitive, and those who wished to be thought so, were commonplace. So accustomed did she become to playing amidst these disturbances that when, some time later, she was asked whether the frequent altercations which took place when late arrivals tried to force their way in did not disturb her, she replied that she was so used to playing amidst shrieks and groans that she scarcely noticed any further noise. The rush to get seats for her performances would start at breakfast time, the crush when the doors opened at six was almost unbearable, but those who managed to fight their way through to a place felt themselves amply rewarded from the first thrilling moment when she appeared. Never had a triumph in the theatre been so complete; never had the Tragic Muse gained such an ascendancy on the London stage.

Mrs Siddons was the mother of five children and the paramount actress of her age. Whenever we were driving past Paddington Green, my mother would point out the statue 'Mrs Siddons as the Tragic Muse'. Unveiled in 1897 by Sir Henry Irving, it was the first statue of an actor, not counting Shakespeare, in London. Here we catch a charming glimpse of Mrs Siddons' more vulnerable side.

His [Sheridan's] enormous charm and humour were seldom displayed for the benefit of his players though he could use them to such effect when he wished that even Mrs Siddons, hard bargainer though she was, let herself be deceived again and again. Once, for instance, she had gone to his house determined not to leave it without the large sum of money he owed her. She came out after some time, reported a friend who was waiting for her, looking 'quite *rayonnante*'.

'Well', said he, 'I hope you have succeeded.'

'Yes, indeed I have.'

'Well, and how was it?'

'Why, you see, we had a great deal of conversation together – he showed me that he is under great difficulties; however, he has positively undertaken to pay me the whole debt next month, provided in the meantime I advance him £50. This I have done, so you see I have obtained my object.'

The Botany Bay of Actors

Sometimes the audience was not respectful. In Leeds, familiarly known as the Botany Bay of actors, a voice from the gallery bawled out, 'That's right...soop it oop, ma lass!' as she prepared to drain the poisoned cup. On another occasion, when it was very hot and Mrs Siddons very thirsty, her dresser sent a boy in haste to fetch her some beer between the acts. He returned when she had already gone on stage and in the midst of the sleep-walking scene from *Macbeth* came up and offered her the foaming mug. In vain she grandly waved him away; he persisted in presenting it for several minutes before the frantic gestures of the stage hands from the wings at last persuaded him to go away. Slopping beer as he went, he hurried off, leaving the audience in such fits of laughter that all Mrs Siddons' powers could not restore the illusion. It was no wonder that after the curtain fell on her final night in Leeds she clasped her hands and exclaimed, 'Farewell, ye brutes!' Proud and indignant she lacked the aplomb of her brother in dealing with vulgar interruptions. Tom Moore recounts how once, when the squalling of a child in the audience was ruining his performance, Kemble walked forward and announced in tragic tones: 'Ladies and gentlemen, unless the play is stopped, the child cannot possibly go on.'

*

Three remarkable women associated with the main events of the French Revolution, are the subjects of the following passages from Women of the French Revolution, *Linda's fourth book.*

1790
The alluring eloquence of Madame de Staël

Madame de Staël was never a beauty. Stocky, with heavy almost masculine features, her chief assets were her handsome arms and bosom, always lavishly displayed. But she made her looks forgotten and inspired an illustrious string of lovers by the fascination of her conversation. It was an art in which the salons of the 18th century excelled, and to which she brought an eloquence and emotional intensity that foreshadowed the romanticism of the 19th. 'If I were Queen,' said a contemporary, 'I would command her to talk to me always.' There were some who found her brilliance exhausting. 'Her works are my delight,' wrote Byron, who knew her in later years, 'and so is she – for half an hour.'

In 1789 her career as a writer – the author of *Delphine*, *Corinne*, and *De l'Allemagne* – still lay before her, though an essay on Rousseau published privately the previous year had won her a certain reputation in the world of letters. But she was already a figure at the centre of events. In her salon at the Swedish embassy all the energy of liberty, as she expressed it, was combined with all the graces of the *ancient régime*. Social barriers to a large extent were broken down, politicians, noblemen and men of letters mingled, though Madame de Staël, always conscious of her somewhat invidious position as the daughter of the Swiss banker Necker, had a special penchant for members of France's noblest and most ancient families, Narbonne and Talleyrand among them

1791
Olympe de Gouges, heroine of the cause of women's rights

Fantasy, extravagance and feminine vanity were lifelong characteristics of Olympe de Gouges. They concealed a strong and original intelligence, and a zeal for justice which was fed by her own sense that she herself had been born to a destiny unworthy of her capacities. From her early career of gallantry she had turned to the world of letters. Through most of the 1780s she had been bombarding the Théatre Français with her plays and having failed to have them staged, had published them with stinging prefaces denouncing actors, management and fellow playwrights. The only one to be performed, *L'Esclavage des Noirs,* a sentimental but deeply felt attack on slavery, was hissed off the stage after three performances – its theatrical failings apart, it is likely that it fell foul of the vested interests of the colonial lobby.

The coming of the Revolution gave a new impulse to

her literary activities. The subject of her plays grew more political and she augmented them with a stream of pamphlets and brochures, proposing a wide variety of social measures – government workshops for the unemployed, a voluntary tax on wealth, improved conditions in maternity hospitals. Strongly opposed to all forms of unjust privilege, she remained a moderate in her political views, seeing in a constitutional monarchy the best hope for France. She admired Mirabeau who returned her admiration, writing gallantly, 'Until now I had thought the graces adorned them themselves only with flowers, but your thoughts are expressed with fluency and backed by intellectual power: your progress, like that of the Revolution, has been crowned with success.'

Such compliments, however, were few and far between. As she bitterly observed: 'I put forward a hundred propositions; they are received; but I am a woman; no one pays any attention.' The fact that her pamphlets were hastily and carelessly written – she herself could barely spell – and mingled serious points with random reflections on her own concerns also helped to make it hard to take her seriously. Her pamphlet *The Rights of Woman*, which at the time aroused little more interest than the majority of her writings, combined in the same way a line of lucid and hard-hitting argument with an irrelevant complaint, in the final paragraphs, against a cab driver who had overcharged her. Two hundred years later, the cab driver, her plays, and her myriad other pamphlets forgotten, the *Rights of Woman* stand out as a prophetic document.

1793
Mme Roland, inspiration of the Girondins

A republican who found herself outstripped by the fanaticism of the left, Madame Roland was arrested on 1 June 1793. Five months later on November 8 she went to face her trial, mounting the stairs that led from the cells below to the great vaulted chamber that was the seat of the Revolutionary Tribunal. She had dressed herself with care, recalled Comte Beugnot, who came to talk to her beside the grille that separated the women's quarters from the men's as she waited for the moment to be called. She was wearing a dress of white muslin with a black velvet sash; beneath a simple bonnet her long hair flowed about her shoulders. Her face seemed more animated than usual; there was a smile on her lips though all those round her were in tears. When the call to the Tribunal came, she turned to Beugnot and squeezed his hand. 'Farewell, monsieur,' she said, 'let us make peace; it is time to do so.' Lifting her eyes to his she saw that he was fighting back his tears, a prey to violent emotion. She seemed touched, but added only two words more: 'Have courage.'

Beneath a statue of Justice in the midst of the hall sat the five judges of the Revolutionary Tribunal, each dressed in black with a tricolour sash and the tall hat plumed with ostrich feathers that were the uniform of their office. Madame Roland took her seat on the bench of the accused on one side of the hall, facing the jury on the other. The proceedings began with the questioning of other witnesses; her manservant, Fleury, her faithful *bonne*, and the governess Mademoiselle Mignot. While the manservant and Fleury stoutly denied any suggestion that their mistress was involved in a conspiracy – for which the first would pay with his head, the second by imprisonment – the governess did her best, in a series of venomous innuendoes, to imply that the Rolands were in the enemy's pay. Her evidence, even in that setting, was too flimsy to be accepted; in any case it was unnecessary. The letters to Lauze Deperret were enough to seal Madame Roland's fate. Her efforts to defend herself, and to justify her husband and the Girondins, were brutally cut short. She was sentenced to be executed that same day.

She returned from her condemnation, wrote a fellow prisoner, with a hasty, almost joyous step, indicating by an expressive gesture the way the judgement had gone. There was just time for her to eat lunch which she shared with another prospective victim, a terrified forger of government bonds, whom she rallied into eating with jokes and kindly words. The prison barber came to cut their hair. She watched her own long locks fall to the floor, and congratulated her companion on his Roman looks when his hair too was shorn.

The execution was timed for mid-afternoon. Arms tied behind her back, she mounted the tumbril, leaning against one end of the cart to remain firmly upright as they made the hour-long journey to the Place de la Révolution (now Place de la Concorde) where the guillotine was mounted. There were few people watching the procession; the day was cold and wintry, too cold to linger outside; famine and the daily struggle for existence had diverted attention from what had become an increasingly familiar spectacle. But at the corner of the Pont Neuf, almost lifeless with emotion, stood Madame Grandchamp. It had been Madame Roland's last request that she would stand at that spot to watch her as she went to her death.

As the cart drew near the place where she was standing there were cries of '*la voilà, la voilà*' from the little knot of spectators gathered there. Fixing her eyes on the figure in white, Madame Grandchamp watched the procession's slow approach. Madame Roland, she wrote, was 'fresh, calm, smiling', a total contrast to her abject companion whom from time to time she tried to cheer. On reaching the bridge her eyes searched the crowd for the face of her friend; a smile and a look showed her satisfaction that she had not failed her at this final rendezvous. Fighting her emotion, Madame Grandchamp managed to remain standing till the tumbril had disappeared into the distance, then, overcome by the violence of her feelings, she all but collapsed; she never knew afterwards how she found her way home.

In the centre of the Place de la Révolution stood a vast plaster statue representing Liberty – the work of the artist Jacques Louis David, it had been erected that summer to celebrate the anniversary of August 10. The guillotine stood further along the square, a gaunt silhouette against the November sky, with a cordon of soldiers at its foot. Here at least a considerable crowd had gathered, with the inevitable *tricoteuses* to the fore. There were chairs for hire for those who wished to watch the spectacle in comfort. Lemonade sellers and news vendors hawked their wares amongst the spectators. The tumbril drew up, the victims descended. Madame Roland faced the insults which were shouted at her with an ironic smile. Thoughtful even now for her terrified companion, she asked that he should be executed first in order to spare him the spectacle of her death. Sanson, the executioner, demurred. 'Surely,' she said, smilingly, 'you won't refuse a lady's last request?' and after a moment's hesitation he agreed.

Unflinching, she watched her companion's death, then in her turn she mounted the short ladder to the platform. As she raised her eyes to David's statue across the sea of watching heads she uttered her famous apostrophe: 'O Liberty, what crimes are committed in thy name.'

*

The next two extracts are from Juniper Hall, *Linda's fifth book. It portrays a group of French aristocrats, among them Madame de Staël and Talleyrand, freshly escaped from the dramas of the Revolution in 1792 to a house in Surrey, refusing to abandon their high spirits and intellectual curiosity at a time when their hopes and ambitions lay in ruins. The priceless gifts of companionship and conversation are a recurring theme throughout Linda's work.*

The evenings were given up to conversation and sometimes to reading aloud. Madame de Staël read extracts from her essay on the passions, which d'Arblay was engaged in transcribing, and blinded them all, wrote Fanny [Burney], with her reading of Voltaire's tragedy *Tancrède*. Fanny was too bashful to speak French in company – unlike her sister she had never been to France – still less to agree to Madame de Staël's persuasions that she should read Shakespeare in return. But she listened, bright-eyed and demure, to the ebb and flow of conversation, the elegant Narbonne, the deep-voiced Talleyrand, 'terse and *fin*', the ingenuous D'Arblay and, animating all with the zest of 'wit, deep thinking and light speaking', the ambassadress herself. 'Ah what days were those of conversational perfection,' sighed Fanny later, 'of wit, gaiety, repartee, information, badinage and eloquence.

In her introduction to Juniper Hall, *Linda wrote, 'The arrival of Talleyrand and other distinguished French exiles, with their alarmingly progressive views, in the quiet Surrey countryside sent a frisson through local society. Fanny Burney and her sister Susanna were both captivated and appalled. "They had wandered out of the sedate drawing rooms of* Sense and Sensibility," *wrote Duff Cooper in his life of Talleyrand, "and were in danger of losing themselves in the elegantly disordered alcoves of* Les Liaisons Dangereuses."'

'How do you like him?' whispered Madame de Staël.

'Not very much,' replied Fanny, 'but then I do not know him.'

'Oh, I assure you,' cried Madame de Staël, '*he is the best of the men.*'

Before long Fanny was forced to agree. 'It is inconceivable what a convert M. de Talleyrand has made of me,' she wrote to her father. 'I think him now one of the first members & one of the most charming of this exquisite set… His powers of entertainment are astonishing, both to information & in raillery.'

*

Despite the difficulties caused by the war with France, young English noblemen continued to travel on the continent just as those who had gone on the Grand Tour before them. One such was Lord Holland who met his future wife Elizabeth Webster in Naples in 1794. At the time of their meeting, Elizabeth was unhappily married to Sir Godfrey Webster and the quarrels of the Websters were becoming common knowledge. However, Sir Godfrey left for England, where he was planning to stand as a parliamentary candidate for his home constituency of Battle, and, pleading ill health, Elizabeth stayed behind. 'To say the truth,' she confided to her journal, 'I made as much as I could of that pretext... as I enjoyed myself too much here to risk the change of scene.'

Elizabeth spent the next year in Italy, with Henry almost always in her entourage. She had taken a house in Florence, a 'delicious residence' in the midst of the Mattonaia gardens, where she entertained three times a week, attracting the leading artists and intellectuals of the town to her salon: the template for the Holland House gatherings was already there. On their evenings alone, Henry read aloud to her; in the daytime they would go on sightseeing expeditions in the surrounding countryside, or travel further afield to visit the galleries and churches of other cities. In Turin, for instance, they visited the chapel of the monastery of St Agnes, with its painting of the saint's martyrdom by Domenichino. 'Lord Holland read a passage to me out of a letter from Charles Fox, from which it appears that he reckons the picture almost the best in Italy', wrote Elizabeth in her journal.

*

Sheridan combined his theatrical career with politics, having been elected Member of Parliament for Stafford in 1780. The following extract from Linda's biography of him gives some background to his work as one of the greatest parliamentary figures of the age.

Sheridan's parliamentary speeches, running to five closely printed volumes, are models of vigour, intelligence and clarity. They might be prepared in bed, where he would retire with box loads of papers and pamphlets and from which he seldom rose till noon, but they represented hours of hard and detailed study. Touching on a wide variety of subjects they were almost always on the side of the individual against the State. As well as his running battle with the government on the conduct of the war and civil rights at home, he spoke against the harshness of the game laws, took on the almost hopeless cause of reforming the Royal Scottish boroughs, where the electoral system, even by the standards of the day, was exceptionally corrupt, denounced the cruelty of bull-baiting and the appalling condition of the London prisons, supported Wilberforce in his campaign for the abolition of the slave trade, and continued to press for fairer treatment for Ireland and the end of discrimination against Catholics. He was assiduous in his parliamentary attendances and constantly besieged outside the House by hard luck stories and petitions. Judging from the fraction that have survived, the number and importunity of the requests with which he was assailed are amazing. Begging letters arrived in an unending stream, asking him to use his interest, now to save a Stafford woman from transportation for horse stealing, now to rescue a poulterer whose stock had been ruined by hot weather, now to fund a plan for reducing the national debt... When added to these were innumerable requests to do with the theatre, his correspondence alone was enough to swamp a lesser, or more conscientious, man. To keep his head above water in politics, and to run, however negligently, London's leading theatre at the same time, was enough for even his ambitions.

*

The next two passages, from Linda's eighth book, Ireland's Minstrel: A Life of Tom Moore, Poet, Patriot and Byron's Friend, *describe the friendship between the Irish poet and the banker poet Samuel Rogers, and between Moore and Byron. As P. J. Kavanagh noted in a review of the book, Moore's sparkling good nature meant that 'nearly everyone he met, fell, in some sense, in love with him, even his opponent in an early duel, and they said so, even the hardest-headed. He could not go on a sea voyage without making a lifelong friend of the captain.' Claire Tomalin went further in her appraisal: 'He charmed a whole society.'*

In the autumn of 1805, a new friend, the most important he had yet met in literary terms, came into his life, the poet Samuel Rogers. With Wordsworth and Coleridge still relatively unknown, and Moore a rising rather than established star, Samuel Rogers was probably the best-known poet of his time... They met with Lady Donegal at her house in Tunbridge Wells and despite the differences in their ages – Rogers was sixteen years older than Moore – were soon on intimate terms. A wealthy banker, with an income of £5,000 a year, Rogers lived in considerable splendour in St James's Street, just around the corner from the rooms in Bury Street where Moore had taken lodgings... His literary breakfasts, at which he gathered most of the leading writers, painters and politicians of the day, were famous; his drawing room, with its Flaxman mantlepiece, red silk hangings and Renaissance paintings, was almost a temple to the fine arts. Pale and cadaverous in appearance – his friends used to call him the 'departed poet' – he concealed a generous heart behind a biting and sarcastic manner; his greatest quarrels with Moore were when Moore, always proud, refused to accept his help when he was in financial difficulties.

A hundred and forty-two of Byron's letters are addressed to Tom Moore; it was to him that Byron entrusted his ill-fated memoirs, and it was he whom Byron wished to be his first biographer. 'He has but one fault...' Byron confided in his journal, 'he is not here.'

By pre-arrangement with the others, Rogers met Byron alone in the drawing room when he arrived; the other two guests then returned and were introduced. Byron was still in mourning for his mother at that time and the colour, 'as well of his dress, as of his glossy, curling and picturesque hair,' wrote Moore, 'gave more effect to the pure, spiritual paleness of his features, in the expression of which when he spoke, there was a perpetual play of lively thought, though melancholy was their habitual character when in repose.'

There was an initial awkwardness at dinner when Byron refused all the dishes he was offered, and asked for biscuits and soda water instead. (His pallor owed something to rigid dieting.) Unfortunately there were none available, but Byron professed himself equally happy with potatoes and vinegar, and 'of these meagre materials,' wrote Moore, 'contrived to make rather a hearty dinner'. But the rest of the evening was a great success, lasting late into the night.

From the time of their first meeting, wrote Moore in his biography of Byron, 'there seldom elapsed a day that Lord Byron and I did not see each other; and our acquaintance ripened into an intimacy and friendship of which I have seldom known an example'. It was an instant rapport on both sides. By 16 November Byron could write to Hobhouse: 'Moore and I are on the best of terms...Rogers is a most excellent and unassuming soul, and Moore an epitome of all that's delightful.'

*

In the first thirty years of the 19th century – when the Whig party was almost constantly out of office – Holland House, the home of the third Lord Holland, became an unofficial centre of the opposition. Presided over by the beautiful and clever Lady Holland and combining discussion of politics and the arts, the salon attracted the greatest liberal thinkers of the age, who championed causes from Catholic emancipation to the abolition of the slave trade. For many of Linda's friends, several of whom lived near Holland Park, Holland House *was a favourite among her books. Thomas Pakenham wrote an acrostic about it on Christmas Day 2018, a few weeks before Linda died. I include it here, followed by a characteristic passage from the text of the book itself.*

'A Christmas acrostic for Linda'

Lord Holland and his plucky spouse
Inspired the world from Holland House.
Nothing survived, the house remains
Demolished by some German planes
And yet we tread the path they took
Immortalised in Linda's book.

1812-1813
Conversational fireworks

Byron hugely admired Sheridan, and the two men, one at
the outset of his fame, the other already a figure of the
past, met frequently at Holland House, where Sheridan,
undeterred by poverty and failure, still took on all comers.
'He was superb!' wrote Byron later. 'He had a sort of liking for me – and never attacked me – at least to my face,

and he did everybody else – high names & wits and orators, some of them poets also – I have seen [him] cut up Whitbread – quiz Me de Staël – annihilate Colman – and do little less by some others (whose names as friends I set not down) of good fame and abilities.'

Lady Holland was in her element amid such conversational fireworks, orchestrating and animating and adding the occasional caustic comment. 'I am sorry to hear you are going to publish a poem,' she remarked to one unfortunate writer. 'Can't you suppress it?' To Rogers, who was writing a book on his travels, she said: 'Your poetry is bad enough, so pray be sparing of your prose.' Her husband, however, took most of the sting from her attacks, bathing all in the sunshine of his genial nature. Witty, well informed and questioning, he guided the conversation with the lightest of touches, and was especially kind to timid younger guests. Like his uncle, he was sympathetic to the 'young ones'.

*

The next passage returns to A Life of Tom Moore

1824
The burning of Byron's memoirs

Five years before he died, Byron handed Moore his memoirs to 'do whatever you please with', provided they were published posthumously. Moore – on the understanding that he would be the book's editor – accepted an advance from the publisher John Murray. But on Byron's death he found himself under intense pressure to destroy the manuscript from those fearful of what it might reveal – among them Byron's executor Henry Cam Hobhouse, and Lady Byron's representative Colonel Doyle. John Murray was also worried that it would be considered obscene — though like the other two men he had not actually read it.

Moore was concerned about how Byron's sister Augusta Leigh would feel, and signed a document promising to give the manuscript to her, but almost at once regretted it. As a compromise, he and Henry Luttrell, another friend of Byron's, agreed with Augusta's relative Wilmot Horton that he could read and censor the manuscript, as could Colonel Doyle. Two days later came a meeting…

The four men – Moore, Hobhouse, Luttrell and Murray – then adjourned to Murray's house in Albermarle Street, and the first-floor drawing room, which was also his publishing office. Horton and Doyle were waiting for them. Horton had seen Mrs Leigh in the meantime, and had completely come over to her side: he was now insistent that the memoirs should be destroyed at once. Hobhouse, triumphantly, accused Moore of misrepresenting Horton; it was only when Luttrell corrected him that Horton admitted he had changed his mind. Moore continued to argue the case for a stay of execution amid taunts and angry barracking from Hobhouse. When Moore, in pointing out the injustice they were doing to Byron's memory in condemning the work unread, mentioned 'as a minor consideration' the injustice they were also doing to him in denying him the benefit of the parts that were not objectionable, Hobhouse exploded: 'This is letting the author predominate over the friend.'… In the end no arguments could save the manuscript. Augusta's wishes, as represented by Horton, and backed by Murray and Hobhouse, overrode the objections of Luttrell and Moore, though Moore went on protesting to the last. Even when the memoirs, and the only copy that existed of them, had been brought into the room and were about to be thrown on the flames, he continued his remonstrances, saying

'*Remember I protest against the burning as contradictory to Lord Byron's wishes and unjust to me.*' It was Horton and Doyle who tore up the pages, and flung them into the fire, both Murray and Hobhouse declining to take part. The fireplace in Albermarle Street, a mute witness to one of the greatest acts of literary vandalism in history, remains unchanged to this day; Byron's portrait hangs over it.

*

The following scenes are from The Young Romantics, *Linda's second book, set in the heart of the Romantic period, when English and French cultures were interacting against a backdrop of turbulent events. 'The originality of the study,' wrote Richard Holmes in his review, 'lies in the degree to which Kelly achieves something like a group biography within such a remarkably short space, not a series of linked portraits, but the evocation of an entire emotional milieu.' The first extract from the beginning of the book sets the tone.*

In the spring of 1827 the Hugos moved house. The little flat above the joiner's shop had been too cramped for entertaining. They found a new apartment in the Rue Notre-Dame-des-Champs not far away, a quiet tree-lined street, still unpaved, and only a short walk from the open fields. Sainte Beuve, whether by accident or design, had moved to the same street a few weeks before. Lamartine, visiting there, was charmed by the peace and seclusion of the new home: 'your mother, the garden, the doves, the peace...which remind me of those gentle priests and country presbyteries I used to love in my childhood.'

No such peace reigned in Hugo's apartment, which was lively with children's voices and with streams of visitors, though a spacious garden behind the house with poplars and an ornamental pond spanned by a rustic bridge gave the illusion of a country setting. Inside he had rented the whole first floor: two bedrooms, a dining room, a study and, most important, a large and handsome drawing room, its walls hung with prints and paintings of the romantic school and, in the place of honour, the golden lily of the *Jeux Floraux* at the Academy of Toulouse, the poetry prize awarded to Hugo in his 18th year. Here in the *chambre au lys d'or*, as it was called, Hugo for the first time had space to receive the growing number of his friends and followers and to found a salon and a school. Sainte Beuve, before long its most assiduous member, would christen the group the Cénacle – the word, deriving from *Cène* or Last Supper, is used to describe a fervent literary or artistic confraternity...

Around Hugo...would gather almost every star, risen and rising, in the Romantic firmament. Not since the Renaissance, as the romantics themselves pointed out, had such a constellation lit the literary and artistic heavens. Here came Lamartine, an occasional and honoured visitor; Alfred de Vigny, blond and aristocratic, who shared with Hugo and Lamartine the triple crown of Romantic poetry; Émile Deschamps, poet, dandy, lover of Spain and Shakespeare, and his brother Antony; Balzac, still little known; Prosper Mérimée; the ebullient Alexandre Dumas; Gérard de Nerval; Théophile Gautier; Alfred de Musset. Here, too, came Delacroix, his polished manners belying his revolutionary reputation as a painter, and with him other artists of the Romantic school: Tony Johannot, the illustrator, whose charming vignettes decorated the poems and novels of the Romantics; the sculptor David d'Angers; Eugène and Archile Devéria; Louis Boulanger, one of Hugo's closest friends, 'an intelligence,' he considered, 'open to Shakespeare and Rembrandt alike'. Musical figures were less common. Hugo had no great feeling for music though Liszt, the prodigy of the Paris salons, would play in his apartment and Berlioz was an admirer and later an acquaintance. Few of the guests had reached their thirtieth year: some, like Musset, were still in their teens. 'It will be remarked,' wrote Dumas in his memoirs, 'that these great revolutionaries were very young.'

The Hugos' hospitality was very simple. Hugo, after early struggles with poverty, kept a close eye on the household accounts. Once Mérimée, a gifted cook, donned an apron to make macaroni à l'italienne, a success, wrote Madame Hugo, that equalled that of his books. More often cups of weak tea were the only refreshment served. 'You had to be all soul when you went there,' said a visitor, 'and leave your stomach in the hall.'

The great theatrical event of 1827 was the arrival in Paris that autumn of a troupe of English players and the ensuing revelation of Shakespeare to French audiences… On a hot night in September, to a packed and curious audience, their first performance, *Hamlet*, was given with Charles Kemble and the young Irish actress Harriet Smithson in the leading roles.

Both Delacroix and Hugo were in the audience that night and so were other young Romantics, Vigny, Sainte Beuve, Gérard de Nerval and Berlioz among them… Few of them could understand English. They perceived *Hamlet* through the mists of translation, taking their French cribs with them to the theatre. But the impression they received was overwhelming. The picturesque costumes, the freedom of construction, the mingling of tragedy and comedy, of violence and lyricism, the death scenes in public instead of discreetly offstage, the naturalism and freedom of the acting, so different from the 'Greek correctitude' of the classical theatre, were entirely new. No doubt the vehemence of the actors' gestures owed something to the fact that they were playing before a foreign audience, but Kemble with his bitter laugh, seeming to reveal a whole philosophy of sardonic disillusion, was an unforgettable Hamlet, and Harriet Smithson – especially in the mad scene – was a heart-rending Ophelia.

A few days later came *Romeo and Juliet*. 'Ah, what a change from the leaden clouds and icy winds of Denmark to the burning sun, the perfumed nights of Italy!' wrote Berlioz. 'What a transition from the melancholy, the heartbreak, the cruel irony, the madness, the tears, the mourning, the lowering destiny of Hamlet to the ardent and impetuous love, immense, irresistible, pure and lovely as the smile of angels, the vengeance, the lost despairing kisses, the fatal conflict of love and death on the part of these hapless lovers! By the end of the third act, scarcely able to breathe, my heart as if gripped by an iron hand, I cried to myself "I am lost, I am lost".'

The young composer fell hopelessly in love. Unable to work he wandered aimlessly through Paris and the surrounding countryside, dreaming of Shakespeare and his Juliet, passing days without sleep, collapsing from exhaustion, once among the corn stooks of a harvest field, once at a table at the Café du Cardinal, where he slept for five hours, to the great alarm of the waiters, who thought he was dead and dared not go near him.

While Berlioz paced the streets in a lover's frenzy, Hugo returned home from the theatre and that very night, it is said, sat down to begin his preface to *Cromwell.* The play was completed and awaiting publication; the preface, imbued with is enthusiasm for the new 'god of the theatre', was published with it in December. It was Hugo's manifesto and would be that of the romantic movement. Sounding the battle cry of 'nature and truth' in the arts, he proclaimed the ideal of drama in the Shakespearean manner – freedom from classical unities and conventions, the mingling of tragedy and comedy, the grotesque and the sublime, obedience to no rules save those of the poet's own inspiration. 'Let us take the hammer to theories, poetics and systems,' he wrote, 'let us fling down this ancient plasterwork which masks the face of art.'

1830
The first night of Hugo's Hernani

Hernani, a poetic tragedy in five acts, was at the vanguard of Romantic drama. The story is set in sixteenth-century

Spain and tells of the tragic love between Hernani, the outlaw chief, for a young woman called Doña Sol de Silva, who has two other suitors...

The three taps sounded. The curtain rose. In a lamp-lit sixteenth-century chamber the black clad duenna hears the knock at the secret door of her mistress's outlawed lover:

> Serait-ce déjà lui? C'est bien à l'escalier
> Dérobé- ...

From the first lines the battle was engaged. With this audacious *enjambement* (the carrying over of a phrase from one line to the next) classical convention was deliberately scorned. From then on the evening was a tumult, 'barbarians' and classicists locked in deadly struggle. 'Brave times,' wrote Théophile Gautier, 'when the things of the mind and the intelligence could stir crowds to such excitement.' Hissed and contested scene by scene and sometimes line by line, *Hernani* and the Romantics nonetheless carried the day. Only the most intransigent of classicists could withstand the charm of Mademoiselle Mars in the final act, in which Hernani, the outlaw chief, by then restored to his rightful rank as Don Juan of Aragon, is about to celebrate his wedding to Doña Sol. 'Dressed in a gown of white satin,' wrote Madame Hugo, 'a crown of white roses on her head, with her dazzling teeth and a figure which was still that of an eighteen-year-old, she seemed a vision of youth and beauty.'

The evening ended in an uproar of approval; only the classicists were silent, not daring to hiss.

The dénouement of Dumas' Antony

The dramatist and novelist Alexander Dumas ranked in fame with Victor Hugo. His love affairs were numerous, his wit and gaiety made him a star of literary salons. He himself knew the value of his ebullient personality. 'If I hadn't been there,' he remarked of a party he had attended, 'I might have found it rather boring.'...

The first night of *Antony* was a success to rival *Hernani*. For the first time an audience drawn from society and the salons flocked to this theatre of the boulevards, the young women with leg-of-mutton sleeves and hair *à la giraffe* in the fashion of the day, the young men with extravagant waistcoats and velvet-trimmed jackets. From time to time the crowd on the pavement would part to let some celebrity pass, a poet or a painter, for the Cénacle was there in force that evening.

The part of Antony was played by Pierre Bocage, a 'fatal' man *par excellence*, melancholy, sarcastic, given to violent access of passion, his air of mystery veiling the gaps in Dumas' characterisation. Marie Dorval, in a muslin town dress, did not please at first: the part of a lady of fashion was unfamiliar to her, her voice was too hoarse, her gestures too emphatic. But as the plot gathered momentum she swept the audience with her. 'The burning passion of the play set every heart alight,' wrote Théophile Gautier. 'The young women were mad with love for Antony; the young men would have blown out their brains for Adèle.' Dumas, a true man of the theatre, knowing that the momentum of the play would be lost if the intervals were too long, hastened the changing of the scenes so that between the fourth act and the fifth the applause had not died down before the curtain was raised again. The last act, the one which Dumas had rewritten for Dorval, ended with the famous finale. Adèle Hervey, discovered by her husband, begs her lover Antony to kill her. He stabs her after a final kiss, and as her husband rushes in confronts him over her dead body: '*Elle me résistait. Je l'ai assassinée.*'...

The famous denouement became part of popular mythology; the humblest Parisian, who had never seen or read the play, could quote the final lines. Some years later, at a repeat performance, with the same two actors, a careless stage manager rang down the curtain too soon. The audience, bilked of their finale, threatened to break up the benches. Bocage, furious at the ruin of his effect, remained sulking in his dressing room and refused to return to the stage. It was left to Dorval to put matters right. The curtain was raised again. Getting up from the sofa on which she had lain as dead, she advanced to the footlights... '*Messieurs,*' she cried, '*je lui résistais; il m'a assassinée!*'

*

In England the political theatre of Holland House was as intense as ever. 'In her study of Lady Holland's Kensington salon,' wrote Jonathan Keates in his obituary of Linda for the RSL review, 'we felt like guests introduced by the shrewdest of habitués.' Here the coming historian of the Victorian age is one of the invited.

1831

Macaulay was a rising man, but a visit to Holland House was an event. 'Well my dear,' he announced to his sister the day after, 'I have dined at Holland House.' The house, he wrote, was delightful, 'the perfection of the old Elizabethan style', Lord Holland 'all kindness, simplicity and vivacity', and Lady Holland 'excessively gracious' to her new guest. But there was a haughtiness in her courtesy, he wrote, which, despite all he had heard about her, surprised him:

'The centurion did not keep his soldiers in better order than she kept her guests. It is to one, "Go" and he goeth, and to another "do this" and it is done. "Ring the bell Mr Macaulay." "Lay down that screen Lord Russell; you will spoil it"; "Mr Allen, take a candle and show Mr Craddock the picture of Bonaparte".'

The first invitation quickly led to others and Macaulay was soon a familiar figure at Holland House, where the breadth of his knowledge and the brilliance of his conversation amazed his hearers. Once embarked on a topic, his flow of eloquence was almost unstoppable; 'he has occasional flashes of silence that make his conversation perfectly delightful,' remarked Sydney Smith. Lady Holland would call him to order with an imperious tapping of her fan: 'Now Macaulay, we have had enough of this; give us something else.'

*

The next four extracts come from Linda's final book, Talleyrand in London: The Master Diplomat's Last Mission. *Talleyrand was France's ambassador in London for four crucial years in the peace of Europe, from 1830 to 1834, when the status of the new state of Belgium was the major consideration.*

Merimée pays his respects

The writer Prosper Mérimée, 29 years old, and already one of the leaders of the French Romantic Movement, spent the winter of 1832-3 in London. Thanks to an introduction to the ambassador – always ready to welcome rising talent – he had ample opportunities of observing Talleyrand in his English setting. He found his appearance disconcerting: 'a big packet of flannel, enveloped in a blue coat, and surmounted by a death's head covered in parchment.' But he was amazed at the position he held in London society:

'I cannot sufficiently admire the profound good sense of everything he says, the simplicity and *comme il faut* of his manners. It is the perfection of an aristocrat. The English, who have great pretensions to elegance and good taste, come nowhere near him. Wherever he goes he creates a court and sets the tone.'

Princess Lieven, wife of the Russian ambassador, pronounces

She had long ruled London as its leading diplomatic hostess, enjoying close if not amorous relations with many of
the leading statesmen of the day – the opposition leader,
Lord Grey, was particularly under her spell, and wrote to
her each morning on heavily scented notepaper. She had
not welcomed the arrival of Talleyrand – politically suspect from Russia's point of view, and a powerful rival so-
cially – and had been quick to denigrate him to William
IV. 'The king asked me what I thought of him,' she wrote
after Talleyrand's first audience. 'I replied that someone
who had spent 75 years of his life intriguing was unlikely
to forget his métier in his seventy-sixth.'

The Lame leading the Blind

Talleyrand's great aim, the alliance of Britain and France,
had been achieved. The phrase *'l'entente cordiale'*, so well-
known in the following century, was first used by Palmerston in the context of the Belgium treaty – he described it
in the Commons as a 'firm and cordial *entente*' – and he
had played at least as great a role as Talleyrand in its creation. It was unfortunate, therefore, that not everyone acknowledged it. It was not only Londonderry who thought
that Palmerston had allowed himself to be manipulated
by the artful Talleyrand. A well-known political cartoon-
ist, 'HB' (John Doyle), made the point in a caricature of
Talleyrand and Palmerston entitled *The Lame Leading the
Blind*. The likenesses were perfect, the foreign secretary
tall and upright, the ambassador limping on his stick, but
there was no doubt who was leading whom. HB's car-

toons, exhibited monthly in London print shops and sold over the counter for small sums, had none of the savagery of earlier artists, such as Gillray, and most politicians took them in their stride. Palmerston, however, was stung by this particular caricature, and according to Talleyrand never forgave him for it. There was nothing he could do about it, he wrote, but it did not make life easier between them.

Once he kept Talleyrand waiting so long outside his door that Grey, embarrassed by his behaviour, came to sit with him himself. In Palmerston's defence, Talleyrand showed scant regard for the foreign secretary's convenience. 'I have never kept him when I could help it,' Palmerston told Granville.

> Other diplomats who want me come and pop into my room... at 12 and come in and go out in a short time; he does not weigh anchor till after one or near two and what he likes to do is to come and establish himself in the armchair at the office about four, just as I want to go away and eat something before I go down to the House of Commons. This I always fight off; for his visit never lasts less than an hour and that throws us out as to everything to be done afterwards.

At the Hollands' salon

Talleyrand had always been grateful to Holland for counting him as 'un des vôtres' in the charmed and exclusive circle of the Whig aristocracy...

Nowhere was Talleyrand happier or more outgoing than at Holland House, with its brilliant cast of distinguished foreigners, artists, intellectuals and Whig grandees. Lady Holland, whose scandalous past – she had left her first husband to marry Holland – meant that she was not received at court, had created her own court, where she could strike terror into timid visitors; a London chemist was said to have invented a special pill for people who had been frightened there. Talleyrand took her with a pinch of salt. 'She pretends to know everything because it makes her look important, and when she doesn't she makes it up,' he once remarked, and when someone asked why she had changed the time of her dinners to the inconveniently early hour of five, said frankly: 'It's just to put everybody out.' Like everyone else, however, he delighted in the gatherings at Holland House.

Two more scenes from The Young Romantics, *again in Paris…*

1835
The first night of Vigny's Chatterton

The play began a craze for suicide à la Chatterton. 'Those were the days,' said Théophile Gautier, 'when poets really did starve in their garrets, and you could hear the crack of solitary pistol shots in the night.' Marie Dorval, who played Kitty Bell, was considered by some as the greatest tragédienne of her day. She brought to melodrama that quality of lyricism which was the essence of Romantic theatre… In Kitty Bell, speechlessly in love with Chatterton, she found perhaps her greatest role. It was a role in half-tints, according with her modest dress in Quaker grey, in which the passions which she had expressed so vibrantly in other parts remained unspoken. In the final act, when Kitty Bell climbs the stairs to Chatterton's room to find that he has taken poison and is dying, the contrast between the violence of her despair and the painful repression of feeling until that moment was almost unbearable. There was a cry of '*Assez*' from the audience. 'I leaned motionless against the box,' wrote Maxime du Camp, who was carried out fainting at the end of the performance, 'a prey to feelings I had never experienced before; and I felt as though I were choking.' Marie Dorval had reserved her most sensational effort for the opening night, her *dégringolade*, or dying fall, from the top of the staircase outside Chatterton's room. She had refused to rehearse it or reveal her plans to her fellow actors, who shared the shock and terror of the audience as she fell back over the banister with an anguished cry and toppled headfirst, arms outstretched, from the top to bottom of the stairs. 'Ah,' wrote Théophile Gautier, 'if only Chatterton could have opened his opium-laden eyes one last time on such an abandon of grief he would have died happy, sure that he was loved as no man ever was and that it would not be long before he met his sister soul below.'

1836
Slim pickings: Hugo's two households

Celebrated for her beauty, Juliette Drouet had first seduced Victor Hugo in 1832 as a young actress with a minor role in his play *Lucrèce Borgia*. Every evening, after the performance, drawn by the promise in her dark eyes, he would go round to congratulate her in her dressing room. It was the beginning of a love that would last for fifty years... But Juliette's place in Hugo's life, though from now on in the wings, was fixed. Two years later he would take upon himself a solemn engagement, regarded by her like a secret vow of marriage, never to abandon her or her daughter. She had won him, said Frédéric Lemaître, by saying, 'You are great'; she would hold him by saying, 'You are beautiful.' Her adoration, her daily love letters to him, 'like so many mirrors,' he told her, 'each reflecting another aspect of your lovely spirit,' held firm, Hugo working to the point of exhaustion to support his two households, Juliette accepting, with almost mystical self-abnegation, the life of poverty and sequestration which he imposed on her. Gone were the lavish silks and laces which had framed her beauty as a courtesan; she was reduced to two or three dresses, much mended and made over. Eggs, cheese and apples were her staple diet, except when Hugo came to supper, when she would prepare a delicious meal, such as he seldom had at home. Adèle, for all her virtues as a mother, was an appalling housekeeper.

*

A final scene from this selection from Linda's books looks forward to the beginning of a new literary epoch.

Among the newcomers to Holland House in the late 1830s was the young Charles Dickens, recently sprung to fame as the author of *The Pickwick Papers* and *Oliver Twist*. It was Lady Holland, ever alert to new talent, who sought him out, though her query to Sir Edward Bulwer-Lytton as to whether Boz was presentable annoyed him by its condescending tone. Dickens, however, was delighted to be invited to Holland House but nervous enough to hope his friend, Serjeant Talfourd, through whom Lady Holland had sent the invitation, would be able to accompany him on his first visit. He first went there – with Talfourd – in August 1838. 'We have had the author of *Oliver Twist* here,' reported Holland to his sister. 'He is a young man of 26, very unobtrusive, yet not shy, intelligent in countenance and altogether prepossessing. It was too large a company of strangers to bring out the fun which must be in him.'

Thereafter Dickens dined at Holland House from time to time, and embarked on an intermittent correspondence with Lady Holland, who was a warm admirer of his work. He once apologized for a muddle over dates – he had forgotten a previous engagement when accepting an invitation to Holland House – on the grounds that he had been distracted 'by some imaginary persons [the Nickleby family] whose affairs have reached such a very complicated pitch just now that they sometimes confuse me in my recollection of my own.'

***

II. Literary Appreciations

Tribute read at Linda's funeral by Thomas Pakenham

Laurence has asked me to say a few words about Linda. I feel very inadequate, although I am proud to say I was involved in their marriage from the very beginning. It was under our billiard table in Ireland, decently hidden under a white sheet, that the happy couple became engaged.

But no one can do justice to Linda's delightful character and her numerous achievements. You have only to look round this church to see how *deep* we all are in Linda's debt. For 57 years she was the devoted heart of a wonderful marriage: loving wife, passionate mother, tireless grandmother, aunt and great-aunt, charismatic sister and sister-in-law – and an inspiration to a huge circle of friends.

'For all her friends and family,' as Valerie puts it, 'Linda has been a rock, an indestructible rock of unselfish love, wisdom and affection.'

What it cost her to perform this rock-like role I can hardly guess. But it was done with such grace and modesty that the performance seemed effortless.

Let me now say something about Linda's career. Writing was in her blood. You could almost say she was born with a pen in her hand. Her father, Ronnie, was a cheerful aesthete, who wrote two novels before he deserted literature for farming and the hunting field – then rediscovered himself as a biographer in old age. Her grandfather, William Camrose, was a newspaper tycoon who bestrode Fleet Street like a pharoah. For Linda, writing was the pursuit she most enjoyed. Someone once said that talking to Linda about a book was like talking to someone about a wonderful party they'd just attended. Skiing and mountaineering were not for her. Apart from pacing the corridors of libraries, she took little conventional exercise. But her desk was her gym. Starting when the children were still at school, she wrote ten sparkling biographies and several delightful anthologies.

To try to write a conventional blockbuster of a biography never, I'm sure, occurred to her. Instead she searched the *shadows* for her subjects. She was a meticulous scholar. And she revelled in the romantics: patiently unpicking the myths that surrounded them, shining a gentle and affectionate light on their follies, but giving them their due perhaps for the first time, when they had been treated unfairly by history.

Her ten biographies were unashamedly romantic and followed an elegant, overlapping pattern. This is the list in the order she wrote them;

Chatterton
The Young Romantics
The Kemble Era
Women of the French Revolution
Juniper Hall
Sheridan
Susanna, the Captain & the Castrato
Tom Moore
The Holland House Set
Talleyrand in London

When complete they covered nearly seventy years like a necklace of sparkling gems. She started with Thomas Chatterton, whose despairing death in a garret in 1770 helped launch the romantic movement. Later she moved to Sheridan and Tom Moore, both irresistible Irish charmers (though both could be called 'Micks on the Make'). Sheridan voted for the Foxite Whigs and was the champion of the underdog, especially the Irish underdog, in the British House of Commons. He was also a hugely successful playwright and ran the best London theatre, although he was outrageously bad at paying his actors. Tom Moore was an early version of a popstar, biographer of Sheridan and best friend of Byron. Of course Moore couldn't save Byron from himself. But his heart-stopping songs helped lift Ireland momentarily out of the mud.

Moving to the French Revolution, Linda stumbled on a nest of wild French exiles incongruously hidden in an English country house, called Juniper Hall, near the Druids' Grove in Surrey. Close by, within carriage distance, lived the exceedingly prim and proper daughters of Dr Burney, including Fanny the novelist. Burney was the tutor in music to George the Third and his family, and close friend of Dr Johnson and Mrs Thrale. Just imagine the culture shock when the delicately reared Burney girls encounter the French. For the French exiles include that voluptuary and master of intrigue, the Prince-Bishop Charles-Maurice de Talleyrand, as well as Mme de Staël, who is having a passionate affair with the former French Minister of War (whom she had recently saved from the guillotine). Fanny falls hopelessly in love with the dashing Captain D'Arblay. To the shock of Dr. Burney, she marries D'Arblay and lives happily ever after.

Juniper Hall, published in 1991, was acclaimed, deservedly, as one of Linda's most original biographies. The book itself has a romantic history. It was selected by PEN to be sent to a group of Russian writers exiled to Siberia. They read it, and were overwhelmed. In letters of thanks to PEN they explained how the sufferings of the French exiles mirrored their own sufferings 200 years later.

For her final cluster of biographies, Linda left the shadows and moved into the glaring light of world politics. After the Orléanists' downfall, the indestructible Talleyrand returns to the stage as the French ambassador in London. Together with Palmerston he cements the *entente cordiale*. And by the late 1820s the haunting issues of the day – Catholic emancipation and the Great Reform Bill – dominate Linda's book on the Holland House set. Lord and Lady Holland are the heroes of the Whig salon which helps propel these vital bills through Parliament. This is their crowning achievement – and Linda's, too.

Let me finish with a quotation from Linda's commonplace book, which was privately printed in 2017 under the title *Consolations*. It comes from Spenser's *Faerie Queen*:

> What if some little paine the passage have
> That makes fraile flesh to fear the bitter wave?
> Is not short paine well borne, that brings long ease,
> And layes the soul to sleep in quiet grave?
> Sleep after toyle, port after stormy seas
> Ease after war, death after life, does greatly please.

*

The Fraught Business of Writing by David Pryce-Jones

Linda as I knew her was a perfectionist, meaning that if she thought something was worth doing then it had to be done as well as possible. Her books have the perfection of works of art, they neither claim too much for the subject nor too little. She was calmly reassuring about the whole fraught business of writing, the solitary occupation that she obviously believed has supreme value. A couple of her projects involved publishing paperback editions of books that had been overlooked somehow. Members of a select committee would meet and make suggestions. It was very rare that she didn't know all about authors and titles obscure to everyone else sitting at the table. An immense range of reading shaped her whole view of the world.

She and Laurence both had an interest in Russia in its Tsarist and its Soviet form. Defecting and then settling in this country, Stalin's daughter Svetlana Alliluyeva soon entered their lives. When Linda then introduced Clarissa and me to her, we found ourselves launched into an extraordinary literary adventure. Svetlana had moved on to the United States but kept in touch through correspondence with Linda and me, and surely others too. Many pages long, her letters amounted to the moving testimony of a lost soul. Linda and I would compare letters and someone one day will surely fulfil the plan we had to co-operate on publishing them.

The custom of this country in speech as in print has always been to make a point by telling a story. Linda herself was one among other masters of brilliant anecdote and gossip. At one particular evening there must have been about a dozen guests, one of them Lord Longford. A lifelong champion of causes, he was in the news because he had been visiting Myra Hindley, the so-called Moors Murderer, in prison. She had convinced him that she was now a changed character. After dinner, the room fell silent as he began to lecture impromptu about her newfound spirituality. It was also perfect when Dame Rebecca West, one of Linda's special fans, stopped him by saying at the top of her voice, 'What a duck!'

*

Scholarship Lightly Worn by Roland Philipps

There is a small bookcase next to my desk which contains the essential works for whatever I happen to be thinking about or writing about: currently a French dictionary, some files of photocopies from various archives, some reference books about the Second World War, a few heavily foxed memoirs, and an edition of the complete works of Saki in eight small volumes. All but the last will move on and others take their place, but Saki will stay as a welcome distraction, a thoroughly entertaining primer in how to endeavour to write sharply to the point, amusingly and with narrative and emotional focus. Linda gave me the edition when I was perhaps fifteen or sixteen, starting to read more widely, considering a career in publishing or journalism, something to do with writing anyway. I wish I still had the note which she wrote to me about them, but can still recall that it spoke of her own love of Saki, as well as his last words.

That thought and generosity in the transmission of her literary enthusiasm was entirely typical of Linda, and I was blessed to be her godson in that and in every other way. Whenever we met, or by postcard, she gave me a brilliant tip, often for the latest detective story or thriller writer she had discovered, sometimes for an out-of-print author who should be resurrected – particularly useful in my first publishing job, sometimes just about someone I might like to read or might be relevant to something going on. And never a dud amongst her recommendations.

My last job in publishing was at John Murray. I was so cheered on my second nervous day, as the first non-eponymous person in my role to walk into the august Albemarle Street drawing-room, to find Linda sitting at a desk, researching her fascinating book about Thomas

Moore in the Murray archives. True to form, she encouraged me to read some of Moore's poetry for myself; something I almost certainly would never have done otherwise. And that book, as with all of hers, was compact but carried a huge amount of scholarship lightly worn alongside her critical acuity, humanity and understanding.

The honour of my being elected to the 'Lit. Soc.' towards the end of 2017 was immense, but made all the more pleasing because Linda was elected at the same time. I am pleased that she went to one dinner, and only sad that her illness prevented us coinciding there: she would have been the ideal member and a marvellous companion.

It was always a thrill to see Linda's handwriting on the doormat. The last book she sent me was one she was throwing out, and was sure I would not want either, but she thought she should try me as I might be interested by its inscription and its connection to a relative of mine. Her unerring instincts were right on both counts. The last two letters I received from her were about my own first book: the first was an introduction to someone she had encountered who was one of only two people still alive who had known my subject, and whose recollections of a lunch-party in Cairo in 1949 brought drama and colour to an otherwise blank point; she had made some speedy connections thanks to her own deep historical knowledge, which were invaluable for me. The second is one I treasure above any other that arrived post-publication: it was generous, perceptive, interesting, kind and witty – the very definition of Linda. I wish she was still here to give her gently unique brand of counsel for my current project, but am privileged and proud to have had her as a literary godmother.

'Franglais' by Marina Camrose

There is no Limerick in French, so Linda and my brother, David Sulzberger, used to play a game of composing them. One limerick celebrated Saint Tropez, who was decapitated:

> Ce curieux bonhomme Saint Tropez
> N'avait aucun chic il est vrai.
> Sans manteau ni fourrure,
> Ni rien d'haute couture,
> Même sa tête était prête à porter.

An expression she was particularly fond of was 'Si t'es pas content, c'est le même prix'. She also liked 'Il ne se prend pas pour une queue de poireau'.

*

In 1986 my parents bought a house in the Lake District, described in Pevsner and with a magnificent vista towards the Vale of Lorton. It was also near to Dove Cottage and we would drive over the fells to Grasmere for the poetry evenings that took place there throughout the summer. My mother became a Trustee of the Wordsworth Trust, then run by Robert Woof who with his wife Pamela became good friends.

The Civilising Force of Poetry and Dining by Pamela Woof

Linda — though I didn't know her well or see her frequently — was a delight in my life. Robert and I visited Linda and Laurence or they came to Grasmere. I didn't realise for a long time how industrious she was as a writer, had no idea how many studies she had published, and all out of her own intellectual energy and imagination, no university to push or pressure her, but a real scholar's curiosity. In making them come alive, poets and singers and courtiers from Chatterton to Tom Moore and Susannah Burney, Linda has made her own place in history.

But it is as a person that I remember her, a presence that brought an air of light and peacefulness to conversations that could have sharp and prickly edges. We admired Laurence for both his skill in language and his knowledge of Russia. Well, I had to certainly, for I was woefully ignorant. Linda made all smooth, and was able to encourage to gentleness Laurence's reception of his students' (mine anyway) persistent ignorance of elements of Russian history – Robert already had a history scholarship at Oxford, so he was well equipped, and Pamela Egremont (often a fellow guest) simply knew everything. We had great classes, as it were, Linda our kind encourager – me in learning, and Laurence in expressing all he felt about the ups and downs of Russian history.

She once warned us when Laurence proposed to recite Pushkin's 'The Bronze Horseman' in Russian that he would weep. We were in a ruined monastery somewhere and Laurence did weep. I knew the poem in English and I understood something of his feeling. I thought it wonderful, and I still do, that both he and Linda acknowledged the place of feeling in the creative arts, that is real and not to be denied or hidden. No other scholar have I known to weep before his audience. That response to Pushkin brought Russia alive to me as nothing else.

Linda also expressed feeling openly and warmly. When we got back from Russia, at some point she gave me a brooch, a butterfly formed of small blue stones, and perhaps a blue enamel, not precious but glittering. It was, as she said, and I knew – a symbol of the spirit, soul – psyche in Greek, a symbol of a kind of unspoken kinship, and I loved to wear it on my dark blue coat. Alas, running for a train, and getting on it as I one day did, I then realised, breathless, that the blue butterfly was no longer on my coat. It must have dropped onto the platform, what with straps and bags around my neck. So like Linda herself now, and like the voice of Laurence in a strange language reading Pushkin amid tears, the butterfly brooch too is a memory. I value them all.

She always praised what Robert set in motion at Grasmere with the Trust and supported its involvement with contemporary poetry, artists and poets in residence, weekends devoted to book collectors, poetry readings, lectures in London; she would have given useful advice with the changes and developments now in train. Institutions must move and try new ways. I hope that some of the old ways will come back, particularly those convivial evenings where people who had listened together to a living poet came and ate together and talked, so that the poetry took on an after-life of diverse response and opinion. The authors were there too, and conversation was often illuminating as well as good-natured. What a civilising force is poetry and dining! Linda was not alone in liking those evenings. Writing needs solitude – Linda knew that; I felt that her alma mater was the London Library. I heard her praise its quietness, privacy, the stacks where you could browse alone yet among such a multitude of minds. The Tuesday evening poetry readings in Grasmere had something of that mingling of the public and the private, an individual response and then a general discussion. I was always glad when I saw that Linda was there.

And in another role, she and Laurence were warm and

wonderful hosts. I loved to go to Lorton Hall, as did Robert. Linda reached out to people and I was lucky in our sporadic and wandering way, to be one of those.

*

'Last Post' by Stoddard Martin (Quarterly Review)

Linda Kelly is a pioneer in the genre of what one might call the non-fiction novella. This is no slighting phrase, nor meant to devalue her quality as historian. If her ten books were to be taken as one, she would be seen as the author of a vast, engaging epic on English and French cultures and their interaction during seventy years of massive change, 1770-1840. In arts and letters, this period is called Romantic, and Kelly has been adept at detailing elements of that phenomenon in theatre, poetry and to a degree music – thus her portraits of Sheridan, Kemble and Sarah Siddons; her evocations of the myth of Chatterton, the life of Tom Moore and the movement of French writers of the Orléanist decade; her miniature of the Burney household during the year of the Gordon Riots. In all of these tableaux the politics of tumultuous times form a backdrop. The dramatis personae are players reacting to dislocation at the top, what Byron labelled 'My friends the Whigs'. Two terms that England adopted from France, *salon* and *liaison*, describe Kelly's milieux. No one is better at portraying them.

The genre she has developed indeed grows out of theatre. Most of her books could be scenarios for a well-made play. There is always deft description of place – a recent title, *Holland House*, was devoted to it – but place is never other than a setting for conversation, interchange of personality and reflection, as in a novel of Henry

James. That said, Kelly is by nature light, her touch free of the ponderousness the James analogy implies. Her drawing-rooms are filled with Voltairean wit more than Rousseauesque meditation. They may exist in a romantic era, but their architecture is classical. Byron comes to mind again, because that *aficionado* of Pope, if never a main character, is the disciple or friend or model of many here – Sheridan, Moore, Hugo – and the chaotic radicalism of his fellow Shelley would be out of place. Politically speaking, Napoleon dominated the era; Kelly, however, never writes about him directly either. *Émigrés* from the *ancien régime* are the subject of one of her books, *Juniper Hall*; and when it comes to politics direct, it is apt that her first full-on portrait should be about that survivor of successive regimes, Charles-Maurice Talleyrand.

The other classical unity of the well-made play is time, and Kelly is exact about it in a book subtitled: *The Master Diplomat's Last Mission* – i.e., Talleyrand's period in London as Louis-Philippe's ambassador to the court of William IV. The Frenchman had been in London earlier in his career, in flight from excesses of the Terror, though his supporting role in the first French revolution made him, Kelly points out, as suspect to Bourbon aristocrats as to the post-Danton Committee of Public Safety. He went on to America, returned to France under Bonaparte, became Foreign Minister and survived into the Restoration to preserve France from utter humiliation at the Congress of Vienna. Not part of the ultramontane tendency around Charles X, he was happy to help in the events of 1830 which brought a 'citizen king' of the cadet Bourbon line to the throne, not as absolutist 'King of France' but as democratic 'King of the French'. This supposedly 'constitutional' formulation appeared or could be promoted as similar to what the English had achieved on deposing the Jacobite Stuarts in favour of (eventually) the Hanoverians. When arguing for the 'legitimacy' of his monarch, Talleyrand was fond of alluding, if with characteristic subtlety, to this precedent.

His mission was firstly to persuade England and Europe that 'the July monarchy' was a good thing and France a stable nation devoted to peaceful continuance of the post-Napoleonic settlement. Successive upheavals in Paris and other French regions, notably the events of 1832 novelised by Hugo in *Les Misérables*, made this task chancy; but Talleyrand cultivated the right people in the English establishment and, helped by his great age (he was now nearly 80), cut a signally unthreatening, civilised figure. In this he was assisted by his niece-by-marriage, rumoured mistress, the Duchesse de Dino, a lively woman many decades his junior, who was well able to manage his household and cauterise wounds. The role-behind-the-scenes of this woman and others – Louis-Philippe's sister, the Russian ambassador's wife, various English hostesses – is sketched in by Kelly admirably. At the same time she leaves us in little doubt of the difficulty of males like Foreign Secretary Palmerston, who once left Talleyrand waiting in his anteroom for so long that Prime Minister Lord Grey felt obliged to come and sit with the old man to reassure him of England's affections.

Grey and Lord Holland, Chancellor of the Duchy of Lancaster, were Talleyrand's great allies among the Whigs; Wellington his mentor among Tories. His role as *eminence grise* behind many of Napoleon's tergiversations was, twenty years after, conveniently overlooked, consistency being the hobgoblin of little minds, especially for survivors. What mattered now, and appears in Kelly's telling to have been Talleyrand's lifelong object, was essential *entente* between the western liberal powers – England and France principally – not least vis-à-vis the *soi-disant* Holy Alliance of the three autocratic powers: Russia, Prussia and Austria. Prime locus for potential conflict was Belgium, a territory that had been Hapsburg before the Revolution, French throughout the Napoleonic period and Dutch by award of the Congress of Vienna. The Belgians wanted neither their current Dutch domination nor return to earlier arrangements; the French wanted Belgium back, but no other European power would accept that; it was Talleyrand's job to square the circle. The heart of Kelly's narrative has to do with how he managed this. The soul has to do with how he later brought himself to relinquish his by then universally-acknowledged position as 'master of ceremonies of his age'.

Talleyrand is a much-written-about figure, and Kelly is complete mistress of the materials that have accumulated about him, including that other great Whig Duff Cooper's biography. She goes back to sources, wishing as she always does to get the *mot juste* in contemporary voice. Of Talleyrand's retirement following a mission that she dubs 'his swansong', she quotes Greville's diary: 'It was fine to see after his stormy youth and middle age, after a lifetime spent in the very tempest and whirlwind of political agitation, how tranquilly and honourably his declining years ebbed away...' It is equally fine to see, after a career spent in capturing lives in the whirlwind of a tempestuous era, how deftly and honourably Linda Kelly continues to add to her epic oeuvre. Before she is finished – indeed, already – we will be able to discern an achievement which, far from being minimal, brings to mind, say, the Tintoretto ceilings of the Doge's palace in Venice or those of Buonarotti in a holier place.

***

III. Personal Reminiscences

Family Memories by Linda Kelly

My mother's memoir, for her family, paints a vivid picture of her wartime childhood. Among the themes to emerge are self-sacrifice, stoicism and a sense of public duty – heroic qualities that she later found in many of the characters she chose to write about.

I was born in Kent in October, 1936, and must have spent the first three years of my life there at Southwood, our house near Westerham. But I don't remember anything of it then and will come to it again with our return there after the war.

My first memory must have been the summer of 1939. It's just a glimpse – a railway carriage and the arm of my father's tweed coat. We were going up to Berwick on Tweed, perhaps because he was signing on with the Border Regiment, where my godfather Francis Law was the colonel. For the last two years everybody knew there was going to be a war, and he had already trained with the Territorials. Now, perhaps July or August, there were only a few weeks to go. I remember walking on the battlements at Berwick, and a Scottish doll my Uncle Francis gave me, also sleeping two in a single bed with Thomas.

The next memory is of the icy cold winter of 1939-40. We were staying at my grandparents' house, Hackwood, where Valerie had been born on November 13 in a room over the front porch. The round pond outside the house was frozen over, and I remember people skating, and trying to do the same, pushing a wooden chair in front of me. Things go blank for the next few months; I do not remember my father's departure for France. But Nursie told me how everyone was waiting for news of Dunkirk at Hackwood; it was hot summer weather and people were sitting on the terrace outside the house. My father's battalion was almost the last to leave Dunkirk, holding the line under continual bombardment while the rest of the army embarked from the beaches. Eddie Robinson, his batman, said it was only due to my father's determination that they all survived. Earlier, as told to me by Robinson, the battalion had been stuck behind enemy lines. Borrowing (or commandeering) a horse, he had disappeared for twenty-four hours to reconnoitre, returning with a route to the coast worked out, which they followed at night in single file and deadly silence. For this, and his conduct throughout the retreat, he should have been given an MC. However, another officer was missing, believed killed. It was thought it would be a comfort to a widow if he was awarded the medal instead, and my father was only mentioned in despatches. Later, the officer turned up. I was told this by my mother for my father never talked of Dunkirk. (There is a partial description of his regiment's part in it in Francis Law's book, *A Man at Arms*.)

As we know, he arrived back in England, dirty, stinking and exhausted; the troops were being sent by train back to their base in the north, but on passing through London, he and Uncle Francis decided to jump ship. They rang up my grandfather's house in Seymour Place, St James's. (The house was later destroyed by bombs; the Berries claimed jokingly that the Rothschilds next door had thrown the incendiary bombs off their roof onto the Camroses'). They were greeted with champagne and hot baths, and my father rang up my mother at Hackwood. 'If you hurry, Ronnie,' she said, 'you can catch the four fifteen to Basingstoke.' Her response – so typically stiff upper lip – became something of a family joke. However, when I asked her about it years later, she said, 'But don't you see, I was longing to see him as quickly as possible.'

Hackwood was full of children – in those days there was a big nursery wing above the loggia and there were nannies and cousins galore: Philip Chetwode, Robin Furneaux, Adrian Berry, Gillian, Thomas, and me; Valerie and Christopher Chetwode were small be-shawled bundles. (Philip, aged just three, earned my mother's undying disapproval by pouring a bottle of calamine on Valerie's face as she lay asleep in her pram.) I think almost all my mother's family were there – my seven aunts and uncles and their spouses, and a number of their friends. Nursie remembered Angie Laycock crying on the terrace, because other husbands, even my father, had returned, and Bob, her husband, was missing. He arrived back later, and went on to a series of heroic exploits, most famous of which was the failed attack on Rommel's headquarters in North Africa.

I have no personal memories of all of this, but it must have been one of the last times I saw my father before we left for America. He always recalls taking me round the private golf course at Hackwood, and how, holding his hand, I would launch myself into space from the bunkers: an example of perfect confidence in him I suppose. Why did we leave for America? Our house in Kent had been taken over by the airforce; Hackwood was shortly to become a Canadian military hospital; my father, presumably, would soon be sent abroad again. One of the deciding factors must have been that my father's brother, Tom, a distinguished professor of paediatrics in Philadelphia, was an American citizen, and he and his wife, Dwight, could receive us when we arrived. Another was that both my parents were devoted admirers of C. F. Alexander, founder of the Alexander method, and the Alexander

School for Children (run by a fearsome woman called Goldie) was leaving for America in July. But discussing it after my parents had both died, Gillian and Thomas decided that the real reason was quite simple: my mother wanted to save our lives. I've always felt slightly ashamed that I didn't fight for my country, though I was only three, but I can't regret the American experience; it was perhaps the happiest three years of my life.

The decision had to be made quickly – Nursie later told me that my mother only gave her a week to decide if she would come with us. We left in early July on a ship called, I think, the Athene; my mother carried a copy of *War and Peace*, given to her on parting by her mother. The journey was uneventful, but the next ship of English children crossing the Atlantic was torpedoed, and after that I think that very few more crossings were made.

I don't remember where we arrived, though I have a vision of the harbour with skyscrapers behind as we approached. My next memory is of travelling – as we had no cot with us Valerie would be put to sleep in the drawer of a chest of drawers lined with blankets. We arrived in Toronto in boiling heat, then joined Miss Goldie's school at a farm in the country. Goldie had droopy golden hair in a bun, and was a kind of crank – both my parents hated the worldly, ambitious attitudes of the Berries, and were suckers for the alternative life style. Luckily Goldie had no power over me; I still lived in Nursie's orbit, and my only memory of the farm is of being chased by a pack of geese, and Thomas, with great gusto, running out with a stick to chase them away. Later we stayed for a while on one of the smaller lakes, Lake Simcoe; the pebbled shores, with trees running down to the water's edge, came instantly back to mind when I got to the Lake District fifty years later.

I think my mother must finally have seen through Goldie, and decided her school was not a very good idea. Anyway, the next place we stayed was Philadelphia, where Tom and Dwight had a large, surburban house with a verandah, with storage space for sledges and logs underneath. It must have been in Germantown, for my first school was a Quaker one, the Germantown Friends. I can't remember anything about it except that the assembly took place in silence; no talking, I suppose so that the Holy Spirit could descend.

We had a wonderful Christmas there. I remember presents – tricycles being hidden under the verandah, and the enormous glistening turkey brought in by the black cook. Soon after this Uncle Tom left for England to serve with the Harvard medical corps, and my mother, for what reasons I do not know, perhaps Dwight was moving house, took us all to Boston. Our first stay there was in a tall dark Victorian house in a terraced street. Our landlady was called Miss Sherman, and was a granddaughter of General Sherman (the one who marched through Georgia). I have only two vignettes of this period: one, an evening gathering where a raven-haired woman in the hall was pointed out to me as Red Indian, the other, an old lady who used to take me to a nearby park to play among the rocks and trees.

I don't think this part of Boston was very salubrious, and the same was true of the local school. Luckily, as I discovered years later, my mother had a grand American friend, Mrs Howard, married to a British husband and also separated by the war, and she helped us find something in a better part of town, Jamaica Plain. Our hosts were called Mr and Mrs Ryder, a friendly, homely couple with an Alsatian dog called Ritzi. They lived in a large, detached, rather Charles Addams house, with a turret and a verandah and steps running down a steep front lawn to the street. The Boston Botanical Gardens were just opposite. Downhill was the school, a low red brick building with a playground, with the American flag on a flagpole behind. I used to feel very proud and British because I was told that as a foreigner I did not have to sing the American national anthem. I also remember feeling proud and British because somehow, subliminally, I had learnt that British children never told tales, and I never did.

The arrangement with the Ryders was that we should have half the house with my mother and Nursie, and perhaps some daily, doing the cooking and the housework. But the yard was common to us all; Ritzi was usually tied up there, and I used to spend hours with my arms around him. Ritzi Ryder was the first dog I ever loved.

We spent the rest of our time in America with the Ryders. The winters were snowy and cold and I remember trying to ski, and on one particularly icy day watching a man crawling on all fours trying to climb the road behind the house. In the summer, when Boston was unbearably hot, we would take a house at Cape Cod. The first year we took one at Catuit with Anne Freemantle and her two sons. She was a rather intellectual lady, with wispy red gold hair in a bun like Goldie, but much prettier. It was a free-standing clapboard house, set a little back from the sea. I don't remember much about the holiday, except that some crabs escaped all over the kitchen floor, with a terrifying scuttling noise, and that Valerie and I had matching blue cardigans with red buttons knitted by Nursie, which we wore after swimming off the long white beach.

The next summer's holiday we shared with Alison Morris, another highbrow lady, with a handsome face and iron grey hair in a bun. (I think buns, like beards, must have been highbrow credentials in those days; I am very glad to

say that my mother always had short brown hair and es-
chewed the droopy, untidy clothes the others wore.) This
time we stayed in Duxbury, a white clapboard house, with
a long outdoor conservatory with mosquito netting rather
than glass over the windows, where we had our meals. It
was an old house, and rather dark inside. There were cup-
boards which led from one room to another, and passages in the rafters, where we used to go and scratch
above our mother's room pretending we were mice – my
mother was terrified of mice. My mother used to read to
us in her room, and it was here she first read us what we
called the Greek Book – the Irish poet Padraic Colum's
adaptation of the *Odyssey* and *Iliad* for children, with illustrations by Willy Pogany. Years later, when I was working
for *Vogue*, I had to talk to Padraic Colum, then very old,
on the telephone in New York, and was able to tell him
how much the book had meant to me. It certainly meant
a lot to Thomas: I can still remember a first poem:

'Thy death', said the dying Patroclus, 'will be soon after mine.'
Said Hector, 'No it won't be for a long time.'

In the garden were tall pine trees – one with a swing
hanging from it which I always think of when I read the
poem 'I remember, I remember' – and, beyond a thicker
belt of trees, the beach. Summer passed in a sunlit haze.

Of course my mother anxiously followed all the news
from the war. Her letters from my father, now in the
Middle East, must have been censored; he was having
quite a jolly time in Palestine and Lebanon, and Mrs
Howard told me later my mother was tortured by fears he
might be unfaithful to her. Money was also a worry, and
Gillian as her eldest daughter shared her fears that it
might run out, or remittances fail to come. The news of

Pearl Harbor seemed a ray of hope to my mother. Now the Americans would come into the war, and long-term victory seemed certain. She began to long to return home, and in the summer of 1943 was offered a place on an aircraft carrier for herself and her family, if she and Nursie would agree to be responsible for a group of English children returning home. All the neighbours in Jamaica Plain gave a farewell party for us; the kindness and generosity of the Americans throughout our stay had been unfailing. The America of our childhood was the *Saturday Evening Post* version, a place of people sitting on rocking chairs on verandahs, of freckle faced Norman Rockwell kids, of neighbourliness and unlocked front doors. For Gillian and Thomas, a little older than me, it was the heyday of Batman and Superman on the radio; no television programme could ever be so exciting.

We had to cut our luggage down to a minimum on the journey. Each of us was only allowed to take one book; I chose Charles Dickens' *Life of Our Lord* with beautiful illuminated gold decorations, but still think with regret of the other books I left behind. I also left behind my first friend, a dark-haired girl called Elaine, and wrote a poem on the subject:

I had a friend called Elaine
And now from me she is ta'en.

We spent our last night in New York; I shall never forget waking up at night in our skyscraper room and seeing the lights of the city all round. We sailed from New York in a convoy, the officers on our ship kindly giving up their cabins to my mother and Nursie and the group of children, some dozen or so I should think, whom they were looking after. We were travelling via Iceland and encountered fearful gales; I remember being thrown from one side of our cabin to the other but never felt the slightest bit sea-sick. There was news that a U-boat had been sighted, but at our age that just added to the fun.

I think we landed at Glasgow. The incredible greenness of the countryside as we travelled to London by train was my first impression of my native land. The other children had been handed over to WVS workers on arrival; we were back together as a family again, tasting our first experiences of wartime inconvenience on the crowded train, where Valerie and Thomas and I spent the night in the luggage racks. It had been arranged that Valerie and I should go and stay with my father's parents, Grandma and Grandpa, while Nursie no doubt was reunited with her family, and my mother with the two older children made arrangements for our next port of call.

My grandparents lived in the middle of Ashdown Forest, a heathy moorland kind of place, like the setting for *Winnie the Pooh*. I remember my grandmother, tall, grey-haired and handsome, coming down the garden path to greet us, with her unmarried daughter, my Aunt Betty, hovering behind. Betty had a squint and was a little backward, but was wholly unthreatening as a result. My grandfather, white-haired with a red nose and bright blue eyes, was a benevolent presence in the background, spending most of his time in his study. Valerie and I stayed in a light sunny room on the ground floor corridor. We don't seem to have been shy at staying on our own, and spent a lot of time rolling down the heather banks to the croquet lawn. As there were no grown-ups to make me eat what I didn't like, I announced to Grandma that we did not eat fish. With rationing at its most stringent – 4 oz meat, 2 oz butter and one egg a week – this must have made catering difficult, but she gallantly rose to the challenge.

After a few weeks with our Scott grandparents, we rejoined our mother with our other grandparents, Moggie and Poppa. Since Hackwood had been taken over by the Canadian army, they had rented a house, Audley's Wood, from the Simmonds family – the Simmondses were big local brewers who had spent some of their fortune in the 19th century in building a large baronial house, complete with (genuine) medieval carved panelling, a massive *porte cochère* and a huge palm-filled conservatory two storeys high. There was a long front drive edged with heavy rhododendrons dividing to make a circle in front of the house, a huge walled garden, and a mass of outbuildings and shrubbery leading to the back drive where we used to play. Inside the open hall, with a broad staircase leading from it, led to a long sitting room with tall mullioned windows down one side and a minstrel's gallery at the end. A door on the left led to the conservatory, and another beneath the minstrel's gallery leading into a tall light room, with windows to ground level, which was the nursery quarters. Upstairs the grandeur of the house subsided into a series of narrow passages with dark pitch pine walls, a little like a Scottish shooting lodge.

Audley's Wood had a floating population: my uncles and their friends on leave, my aunts, Diana with the Wrens, Sheila and Patricia with the WVS – coming and going in their smart dark uniforms. My father was still away, but there was one encounter which would be significant for our immediate family later. Ivor Williams was a neighbour: his father Colonel Williams, a veteran of the Boer war as well as of the First, lived at Hartley Whitney. He and Diana had been great friends, going to teenage parties together, and playing various japes around the countryside. He had joined the Grenadier Guards as soon as he was old enough, and had been very badly wounded in Italy, where he got an MC; much of his face had been burnt, and he spent two years in hospital having it rebuilt by the great plastic surgeon Archibald McIndoe. When he came out it was still very badly scarred, and he was naturally self-conscious when he came to tea at Audley's Wood soon after. However, Juliet – Sheila's daughter, who must have been about two – took a tremendous fancy to him, and insisted on sitting on his lap throughout, which must have helped his confidence enormously.

I don't remember much of those on leave, but Freddy Birkenhead must have been there before setting out to join Fitzroy Maclean with Tito's guerrillas in Yugoslavia. Years later another, junior, member of his group told me that Fitzroy insisted on having high-profile people with him – perhaps to raise the influence of his mission. Anyway, Freddy as an earl was one, the others were Randolph Churchill, considered almost unemployable elsewhere, and Evelyn Waugh. (Waugh's description of Fitzroy was 'dour, unprincipled, and possibly very wicked'; to the rest of us he was always a hero and his *Eastern Approaches* a classic of the 20th century.) Sheila gave Freddy a copy of the Bible before he left. At one point he and Waugh and Randolph were holed up in a cave together. Randolph talked incessantly and in order to try and shut him up they bet him that he could not read the Bible from end to end. Thereafter there was silence, broken only by Randolph's occasional exclamations as he read through the Old Testament: 'God, what a shit God is!'

Seymour and Julian were both in North Africa and later Italy, Julian having been a commando and achieved the distinction of being the youngest major in the army. Rodney had been wounded in the thigh, and had shared a ward with the great air ace Douglas Bader, who had gone on flying though he had lost both legs. Rodney had stories of how Bader used to escape from the ward sister, propelling himself down the passages on a hospital trolley driven at top speed.

Another friend of the family was Basil Dufferin. He was a great-great grandson of Richard Brinsley Sheridan, as I learned years later, and, like Sheridan, liked nothing better than romping with children. Whenever he arrived, he would leave the drawing room to come and play with us in the conservatory next door. He was later killed in Burma. He was the only person I knew who was killed in the war, and I used to pray for him each Remembrance Day: I still do. John Betjeman (Patricia's brother in law) wrote a poem, 'In Memory of Basil, Marquess of Dufferin and Ava'. I shall allow myself to quote a few lines.

> …On such a morning as this
> with The Times for June the eleventh
> Left with coffee and toast
> you opened the breakfast-room window
> And, sprawled on the southward terrace,
> Said, 'That means war in September.
>
> Friend of my youth, you are dead!
> and the long peal pours from the steeple
> Over this sunlit quad
> in our University city
> And soaks in the Headington stone…
>
> …Stop, oh many bells, stop
> pouring on roses and creeper
> Your unremembering peal
> this hallowed, unhallowed V.E. day, -
> I am deaf to your notes and dead
> by a soldier's body in Burma.

As with many families in the war, with fathers away, and mother perhaps working, the children were often clustered together under some relation's wing. My grandfather, Poppa, spent most of his time in London, where – his house having been bombed – he and Moggie had taken rooms in the Dorchester. He had been, I think, Minister of Information for a short time, until removed thanks to the intrigues of Beaverbrook (see Michael Hartwell's book on his father), and was running *The Telegraph* on a skeleton staff. Before the war he had been ill at the time of the Munich crisis. Seymour had run it in his absence and was responsible for the paper's brave and honourable stance against appeasement. Till the end of his life my father would never take *The Times* because of its craven behaviour at the time of Munich.

Moggie, formidable, with jet dark hair swept up like an Edwardian beauty, usually accompanied my grandfather to London, and the household arrangements were nominally in the hands of my great-grandmother, Granny Corns. She was a frail, slight old lady, who boasted of having had a seventeen-inch waist when she was young, and was teased by her grandchildren because she used to read romantic novels disguised by a brown paper cover. She was a little twittery and silly; my grandfather's patience used to be sorely tried when she would read him extracts from the *Daily Mail* (the Rothermere family were our great rivals) at breakfast. But my mother, who was somewhat left out as the other children came along, loved her dearly; Granny Corns taught her to knit, and when she first went to Roedean and was miserable and rather homesick, used to send her notes and little gifts to cheer her up. When Granny Corns was a young girl she had met an old lady who had been at the Duchess of Richmond's ball on the eve of Waterloo, a link with the past that brings it very near.

We had a marvellous time with our cousins when we first arrived at Audley's Wood. Robin founded an organisation called the Bad Boy Scouts, whose aim was to do one bad deed a day: I'm not sure if he succeeded, but we certainly had great fun. But shades of the prison house began to close. Poor Gillian, with pudding basin hat and pigtails, was sent off to Priorsfield, a tough boarding school where she, accustomed to the friendliness and easy-going ways of the States, was miserable. Thomas, a little older than Robin and Philip, went to Hawtreys, a prep school in Wales; I can see him now, or am I imagining it, his face pale, his shoulders bravely braced in his bulky grey school coat. Luckily, I think he didn't hate it nearly as much as Gillian loathed Priorsfield.

With Thomas gone, I lost my earliest companion; of course I went on seeing him in the holidays, but our lives were so different that the old closeness was lost. Meanwhile, Robin, Philip and I joined a class of local children, who were taught by a tall, red haired governess, Miss Dwire. Different families took turns to house the classes. We began in the dining room at Audley's Wood, then moved to Dummer, where Marian Fergusson's two nieces, Hermione Faulkner and Sara Wignall, were staying for the war. (Hermione's mother was twice widowed in the war, Sarah's had died when she was three.) Sarah leaves an account of this period in her book *A Place of Shells*. She married Michael Alexander, and died from an overdose after a series of nervous breakdowns. She left two exquisite books, written under the name of Sarah Fergusson, and has now become something of a cult figure among feminists in America, a kind of poor man's Sylvia Plath. After Dummer, the class moved to the Portsmouths' house at the top of Farleigh Hill, where Philippa Wallop and her younger sister Jane shared our lessons. They were always beautifully turned out; I remember them with pearls and black velvet dresses at children's parties.

I suppose Audley's Wood must have been too crowded for all of us to stay there permanently, and my mother soon rented a house called Skippetts close by. It was a white 18th century house, said to have been a smuggler's hideout, with a huge cedar outside, a mellow brick-walled kitchen garden, and an iron fence separating the lawn from the field beyond, which in summer was always covered with roses. There was a little wood, or shrubbery, by the side of the kitchen garden, where we used to climb and build houses, and through a gate by the side of the field a bigger, more mysterious wood where we seldom ventured. Like everyone at that time, we kept chickens in the back yard, and used to go gleaning in the corn fields for their food; it was here I first encountered a prisoner of war, a small russet-faced Italian who was working on the nearby farm, and always waved at us in a friendly way. Perhaps he had children of his own at home.

I used to catch the bus up Farleigh Hill, by a pub at the end of the lane; Robin and Philip got on one stop earlier from Audley's Wood and were usually to be seen rolling around fighting in the back, till the conductress threatened to throw them off. Although I was very much of a tomboy I was beginning to find that boys were too rough, and avoided physical conflicts if I could.

Once we were installed at Skippetts my mother took a job at the Red Cross second-hand shop in Basingstoke. There were lovely things brought into the shop, and my mother bought me Perrault's fairy tales, with magical illustrations by Edmund Dulac, and the equally magical Hans Andersen's fairy stories illustrated by Kay Nielsen. These two books were indisputably mine; many of the others were recycled for birthdays from one child to the next, so that later on there were great arguments about who they really belonged to, Gillian who had been given them first, or Valerie who received them last. As the one in the middle I was in a weak position.

We were still at Skippetts when my father returned from the Middle East. I came down to breakfast one morning, and there he was. My first memory, which I used to tease him about, was of him complaining about the tea. He was so used to the strong army version, made with condensed milk, that the ordinary kind seemed tasteless. I think he was only there on leave: he was attached to Bomber Command in Sussex (and against all orders flew with the gunner on one of their big bombing raids to Germany, leaving a note behind in case he didn't come back.) He must have been in London from time to time too for he used to bring us Rider Haggards back from the London Library – how we thrilled to *She* and *King Solomon's Mines*.

We left Skippetts for Southwood, our old home, shortly before the war ended. Most of the pilots who stayed there had been killed in the Battle of Britain; they used to have wild parties in the evenings, letting off pistols so that the walls were marked with bullet holes. My parents always used to say that the thought of their deaths made the house a sad place after their return, but we children loved it. A late Regency house in yellowish brick, it had a verandah in front and a circular drive with a monkey puzzle tree in the middle. At one side of the house there was a corrugated iron bomb shelter: no vain precaution, for there was a huge bomb crater in the field across the drive. Despite the occasional warning of V2s or doodlebugs we never actually used it as a shelter; my father later tried unsuccessfully to grow mushrooms there. At the back of the house there was an orchard, and a garden path leading to the electric light plant, a small brick house where the electricity, which often went wrong, was made. Beyond that there was a belt of trees, with steeply sloping fields and woods beyond. Southwood was a paradise for children, with chalk pits and fascinating hollow trees where one could hide.

From the main drive of the house a drive led sideways down an avenue of cherry trees to the stables and garage, a dream of pink blossom in the spring. In the field beside it there were my father's two hunters, Spitfire and Amanda: Spitfire, black and fairly heavily built, born at the time of the Battle of Britain; Amanda, a beautiful thoroughbred bay. Her mother Celandine, a chestnut thoroughbred and my father's favourite horse, had died from neglect in the war. In a cottage by the garage lived the groom, a rather shifty man whose name I can't remember, and in the lodge at the end of the drive were the Birds, who had first come to my parents from my grandparents' house at Barrow Hills, when they got married. My father was devoted to Bird, who like him loved animals, and kept a picture of him on a horse on the mantelpiece of his dressing room at Huish after he died.

Poor Gillian and Thomas were already caught up in the boarding-school system, though Gillian had been moved from the horrid Priorsfield to a cosier and more eccentric school called Hampden House. I went to a PNEU school in Oxted, about five miles away; my father used to drop me there on his way to the station in the mornings, and in the afternoons I would take the bus back up to the top of Westerham Hill, then walk the last three quarters of a mile or so along a little lane, playing at dodging German spies in the hedgerows on the way.

When V.E. day took place my grandfather was the only

person besides Churchill's family to dine with the Prime Minister after he had greeted the cheering crowds in Trafalgar Square. After V.J. day at the time of the final victory, the King sent a personal message to every school-child in the country, perhaps the Empire too. It was an illuminated piece of paper, and I can still remember the first lines:

> Today, as we celebrate victory I send this personal message to you and all the other boys and girls at school. For you have shared in the dangers and hardships of a total war and you have shared no less in the triumph of allied nations. I know you will always feel proud to have belonged to a nation which was capable of such a supreme effort, proud too of parents and elder brothers and sisters...

My memory stops here, and the message which was framed, has long since disappeared.

I can't remember the date on which the 1945 election took place, but I remember Thomas, with whom I shared a room, coming up from supper to say that Labour had won. It seemed unbelievable; throughout my conscious life Churchill had been Prime Minister, and the natural order of things was now reversed. But I'll always remember the sunny evening of September 6 when I met my father coming up the path beside the cherry avenue to say that I had a baby brother. At first Nigel was just a bundle in a shawl, later a little figure at whom I used to make faces and play peek-a-boo through the bars of his cot. Valerie, who'd always been the baby, now went to school with me, distinguishing herself by her prowess at running and jumping in the school sports.

It was a lovely school. The PNEU system was originally devised for families abroad. It was thorough and imaginative – we studied a different artist each term for instance, and kept century books, which showed all the costumes and inventions of each century – and there were exams at the end of every term so exams never held much dread for me. After school I would rush home to listen to Dick Barton, Special Agent on the radio. The episodes always ended at some thrilling moment with the hero and his friend Snowy being tied up in the cellar, or trapped by a rising tide, and I could scarcely wait for the roll of drums which heralded the next instalment.

Southwood was a happy place for me. The atmosphere and surroundings were much like those in *Just William*. We would play in the woods and fields, and go back to tea with our friends in their houses, usually Edwardian and detached, with large gardens round. One of my friends, Anne Clark, was the daughter of the script writer for the famous Ealing Comedies, *Kind Hearts and Coronets* and *The Lavender Hill Mob*. But it was not a good time for my mother. Going through Harrods Food Hall one day on the way to buy some baby things for Nigel, she slipped and hurt her back, and was confined to bed for months. I used to have a fantasy that if only I could spend one day without sin, she would get better; it's amazing how difficult it was – even at my comparatively innocent age and with few temptations, I never achieved my aim.

Maybe it was the feeling that Southwood was unlucky, as well as the fact that my father – who had carried a London Library copy of *The Principles of Dairy Farming* all through the war – wanted to farm on a larger scale, that made us move to Hampshire. My grandmother had heard of Huish, a house and 200-acre estate adjoining Hackwood, clinching my parents' decision to move by telling my mother if she didn't take it her brother Julian would.

They spent the autumn of 1947 carrying out the move.

There were no spare coupons for carpets or curtain material, but my mother found some kind of pink and blue blanketing that wasn't rationed for the bedroom curtains. The carpets and some other curtains were moved from Southwood, but the drawing room curtains were not – just as well since they were state-of-the-art 1930s, with modernistic zigzags – and wouldn't have gone at all with a solid Edwardian house. My father did most of the carpentry and electrical work himself – it was almost impossible to find tradesmen at the time. The garden was much overgrown, but when we first moved there were remnants of what may have been a Gertrude Jekyll design, brick steps leading down to round lily ponds (soon filled in as being dangerous for children) and an elaborate water garden with little channels and islands leading from the stream. There was a dog's graveyard by the side of the drive. The stables and garage were full of lumber and rubbish, and I remember coming across the pages of a torn poetry book among them. Four lines still stick in my mind, I don't know who they're by:

> And a feeling of sadness comes o'er me
> That is not akin to pain,
> But resembles sorrow only
> As the mist resembles rain.

I won't go on to describe the house, only stopping to recall rushing excitedly along the passages at the beginning of school holidays, and the big teenage dances, with a band at the top of the steps in the drawing room when I got older. In January 1948 I went to Southover Manor, a school in Lewes, fronting onto the street, with playing fields and gardens running down to the railway line behind. I always think, rather fondly, of school when I hear a train in the night. Remembering my mother's unhappiness at Roedean, and Gillian's at Priorsfield, my parents were determined that my experience should be different. It was a nice, unambitious school mainly frequented by the children of the country gentry, perfectly pleasant once one got used to it but not very stimulating. I remember long acres of boredom, of longing for real life – as represented in all the Georgette Heyers I used to read – to begin. I suppose the spirit of the school was summed up by the fact that we all had to learn to play the National Anthem, even if we hadn't had piano lessons. The idea was that when we grew up we would probably marry the squire and have to play it at the local Women's Institute.

Enough of the boredom of Southover; once I entered my teens and stopped playing in the woods and climbing trees the holidays were pretty boring too. I would crouch by the electric fire in the sitting room, reading Agatha Christie and waiting for the gong for the next meal to ring. Every morning at nine-thirty I went hacking for an hour with my father, a process I endured rather than enjoyed. There was a heavy brown pony with a hogged mane called Blaze, impossible to stop or control on the occasional times when I went hunting, and I lived in terror of committing some solecism. Hampshire parties were quite fun but I never felt I belonged to the smart set, and one of my great bonds with the Makins was that they felt they didn't either. Mollie, even then, managed to straddle both worlds.

During those teenage years I began to get the outlines of my family straight. I used to see my Scott grandparents every term, since their house was near enough to Lewes to go there for lunch on Sunday on the half-term weekend when my parents came down to visit. My grandfather would show me his collection of netsuke – Japanese knife holders in elaborately inlaid metal – and talk endlessly to my father about the situation in Malaya, where the family firm, Guthries, had been the Singapore equivalent of Swires or Jardine Matheson. A McNair ancestor had designed the cathedral and Government House in Singapore, and my father's grandfather Thomas Scott had been the moving power behind building the docks. Sadly, my grandfather had been bought out of the Guthries by an unscrupulous partner, and had subsequently lost a lot of money on the rubber market. He was a very unworldly man, who had been brought up by a private tutor, who even accompanied him when he went to Cambridge. Here he got a first in classics, following it up with a first in medicine at Edinburgh. He never practised medicine, except during the First World War, when due to his advanced age – he was in his forties – he was known as Grandad by the patients.

On the occasion of my grandparents' golden wedding we all went to a lunch at a hotel in Crowborough nearby. It was a sunny day, and my grandfather recalled how in his young day, men who got engaged used to consult Proverbs, chapter 11, by shutting their eyes and putting their finger on the page. The verse it landed on would describe the qualities of their future wife. In Grandpa's case it told him: 'The price of a good woman is above rubies.'

My father has written about his parents in his family memoir. My grandmother had been half Swedish; I remember her showing me the picture of a white house by a lake, just like something out of Ingmar Bergman's *Wild Strawberries*, where she used to spend her childhood holidays. She also told me a story about some Swedish relation who was given a bad oyster when sitting next to the King of Sweden at dinner. Being too polite to spit it out, she swallowed it and died.

Tom and Dwight came over from America with their children to stay with us in the hot summer of 1949. Tom was already a leading figure in paediatrics. His skills would turn out to have a particular meaning for us, for in 1936, when Thomas Pakenham was three, he developed polio. Tom, who was then working at St Thomas's, visited the Radcliffe Hospital in Oxford once a week, and it was he who recommended the right treatment. Dwight was, I think, the first woman professor of biochemistry at Harvard. My mother always used to say that Tom was remarkable, but Dwight was close to genius. They were the most approachable people I have ever met, utterly oblivious of age or station.

Leslie, my father's younger sister, had also been much sought-after in her youth, with admirers including Mortimer Wheeler and Nigel Nicolson. Leslie studied as an archaeologist, I think at London University, and married a fellow archaeologist, Peter Murray Threipland. He had large estates including the romantic Dryburgh Abbey in the borders. I remember staying with them once in their house in Caithness, where I tried on a dress which one of Peter's ancestors had worn at the ball for Bonnie Prince Charlie in Edinburgh.

Although we saw quite a bit of our Murray Threipland relations, our proximity to Hackwood meant we saw far more of our relations on the Berry side. It is impossible to describe the glamour of all those aunts and uncles in their prime, when you saw them in the great dining room at Hackwood (only used for New Year's parties in Seymour's time) with Poppa presiding at one end. Sometimes there were distinguished visitors, among them Brendan Bracken, Professor (Lord) Cherwell and Winston Churchill, whose painting of the Cathedral, the great beech avenue in Spring Wood, used to hang in Seymour's study. Seymour, back from the war, with his sleek dark hair and saturnine features, was the handsomest man you ever saw; Freddy looked like Scott Fitzgerald; Diana with her snapping dark eyes and slightly mischievous expression was at the height of her good looks. It was the time of Dior's New Look and Gillian, seventeen and just out in the world, looked ravishing in a swishing black taffeta skirt with a cinched-in waist. But of course, it was my grandparents who dominated the scene.

Poppa first. The story of the three brothers from Merthyr Tydfil who each became peers and made their fortunes is a romantic one, but it wasn't completely rags to riches. Poppa's father, John Matthias Berry, was Mayor of Merthyr, and a prominent local citizen. He was an ardent Liberal – Poppa was called William Ewart after Gladstone – and worked as an election agent for the Liberal MP, D. A. Thomas, later Lord Rhondda. Gwllodygarth, his house outside Merthyr, was a substantial, rambling place, run on strict God-fearing lines: my mother recalls that one was never allowed to read a novel on Sundays. Nonetheless, Poppa left school at fifteen, working first as a reporter on the *Merthyr Times*, and left for London with I think £50 in his pocket.

I like to think of the gaslit London of the late 1890s, of landladies and music halls and boxing matches. My grandfather's first journalistic venture was the *Boxing Times*. Very soon he was doing well enough to send for his brother Gomer. I remember Gomer telling me that he and Poppa ran the paper single-handed, but that in order to give the impression of having a larger staff Gomer called himself Mr Gomer when selling advertising. One client smelt a rat. 'You look very like Mr Berry,' he said. 'Ah, well,' said Gomer, 'all Welshmen look the same.'

My grandfather was very loyal to those he encountered on his way up. There was a flower lady from whom he used to buy a button-hole each morning; when he acquired the *Telegraph* he asked her to do the flowers for the building.

Many of Poppa's friends were artists and journalists. One of them was the painter James Pryde, and it may have been he who did the drawing of Poppa on the night before his wedding: 'Goodbye Bill Berry Bachelor'. Poppa first met Moggie's family when he was staying at the Tregenna Court Hotel in Cornwall. His elder brother Seymour was suffering from TB, and Poppa had taken him down there to recover in the bracing seaside air. Moggie's father, Thomas Corns, was also staying there, and after they returned to London asked Poppa to dinner at his house in Bolton Street. Moggie was in America; against her family's opposition she had taken herself to Radcliffe College, Harvard.

Moggie was a strong personality. She was a women's suffragist (the non-violent arm of the suffragette movement) and years later once rebuked Winston Churchill for his opposition to the cause. She was a Theosophist, a follower of Annie Besant, and like her daughter Diana had psychic gifts. She played hockey for England and was a crack revolver shot; at the beginning of World War II when some of Seymour's fellow officers were showing off their prowess with a pistol, she picked it up and fired three bull's eyes at the target.

Poppa went on meeting the Corns family and shortly after Moggie's return from the States the two became engaged, marrying in a registry office (Moggie considering a conventional church wedding hypocritical) soon after. Early in 1906 they went on a tour of America. Leaving Moggie, who was heavily pregnant, at a hotel in New

York, Poppa set out on a tour whose last stop was to be San Francisco. While he was away, my mother was born prematurely, arriving in such a rush that the hotel staff had to deal with the delivery. Poppa hurried back to be with her, a decision that may have saved his life, for the San Francisco earthquake began on the day he had been scheduled to arrive there. Gomer, who did not know of the change of plan, was desperate with worry till a laconic cable arrived: 'Safe Bill'. He was so overwhelmed that he fell on his knees in thanksgiving on the office floor.

In the 1930s my grandfather had to fight an epic battle with the Harmsworth press, who were determined to break him. Apparently, Lord Rothermere had been infuriated by the fact that the Amalgamated Press, the Berrys' newspaper empire, was listed as the largest in the world. He started a vicious battle, opening rival newspapers in all the provincial towns where the Berrys' had papers, often suborning their staff, either by luring them away or paying them to pass on confidential information. Needless to say, Moggie was right beside Poppa in encouraging him to fight, though they now had eight children and had everything to lose. But Poppa and Gomer won through thanks partly to the support of the Westminster Bank, Temple Bar. Seymour tells the story of how Brendan Bracken, then a henchman of Rothermere's though later a friend of Poppa's, came to the manager of the bank telling him, as a matter of friendly advice, that he should withdraw the Berrys' credit as they were bound to lose. The manager listened to him politely, asked him to repeat the advice, which he did, then told him: 'There is the door.'

By the time I saw Poppa after the war he and Gomer had divided forces, Poppa keeping the *Telegraph*, the *Financial Times* and the Amalgamated Press, Gomer the *Sunday*

Times and various other papers. Till 1930 the two brothers shared a bank account – Seymour, the eldest and Poppa's favourite, had been killed in a riding accident in 1926. But Gomer, who had been widowed, had – in 1931 – remarried a worldly and ambitious divorcee, Edith Merandon du Plessis, who was determined that Gomer should no longer play second string to his elder brother. Poppa's children did not get on with the Gomer cousins – Randolph Churchill later christened them the Good Berries, Gomer's being the Bad Berries – and it seemed time for a break to come. After Poppa's death Gomer sold the *Sunday Times* behind Michael's back, which led directly to his founding of the *Sunday Telegraph*.

I did not know Poppa as well as my Chetwode and Birkenhead cousins who used to stay at Hackwood, rather than just coming over for tea or dinner as we did. But I remember my feeling of pride when after being in a road accident – I had been knocked over by a motor bike – I admitted at dinner that it had been my own fault. 'Well done,' said Poppa from the end of the table.

I also remember thanking him in the hall at Hackwood for giving me a coming-out ball at his house in Carlton House Terrace. He squeezed my hand. It was the last time I saw him. Shortly after he went to hospital, but I was able to write to him and thank him after the dance before in died on June 15, 1954. His last words apparently were to thank the nurse for bringing him a cup of tea.

Moggie lived on till 1962. She and Poppa had been incredibly close, and she followed all his business affairs. It was she who recommended Desmond McCarthy as the literary editor of the *Sunday Times*, and someone recalled how she and Poppa would look through the *Telegraph* each morning, often needing to do no more than exchange a glance in comment. I must just end with a story I was told by someone who had known Poppa as a young man – Poppa was always very kind to young people. He asked him what was the secret of his financial success. 'You must buy cheap and sell dear,' said Poppa, ' – and it's not as easy as it sounds.'

With Moggie's death things changed at Hackwood. Only a few months after she died her son Rodney – 'the honourable Rod' as his friends used to call him – had died after an operation on his hip. Tall, bespectacled, with a big Roman nose, he was less clever and glamorous than his brothers and sisters, but probably the kindest of them all. It was lucky that Moggie was spared this loss. Some of the Hackwood contents were divided after her death and there is a picture of the now only seven brothers and sisters on the terrace outside the house after the division. There was never the slightest argument among the brothers and sisters over the dividing up, except for certain dark hints that Diana had taken the precious set of Rupert books which had mysteriously disappeared from the nursery. Years later Valerie rang me up from Ireland with the thrilling news that the Ruperts had been reprinted by Woolworth's and were on sale in Mullingar.

By the time Poppa died I was seventeen. I had finished my schooldays at Southover, having stayed on an extra year since thanks to a Socialist directive no one was allowed to take their O-levels till they were sixteen. I and two other girls whose birthdays came too late stayed on to take them, and I was able to do A-levels in French and History at the same time. It was a very happy year: school seemed home from home by then, and I enjoyed the work, particularly French literature. The ethos of the school (that of the girls, not the teachers) was never to try hard at anything. But I did try quite hard during this year, and after I left I was awarded two prizes, one a special prize for history, and one for the best exam results of the year. But by the time I got them they no longer had much meaning. I was now at a finishing school and embarking on the difficult process of being grown up or, as my father's poem put it, beginning my own unaided pilgrimage. Of course, this wasn't really true, my parents always went on helping me. But childhood and its simplicities were over and I was entering uncharted territory.

***

Remembering Linda by Valerie Pakenham

Linda was born on the 1st of October, 1936. I was born three years after her at Hackwood Park, our grandparents' house outside Basingstoke, in November just at the beginning of the war. It must have been an awkward event for our mother, with a husband already enlisted and three small children to look after. She had already had to evacuate their house in Kent which was just beside Biggin Hill, an airforce base and obvious target for German bombs. In 1940, our father narrowly escaped from Dunkirk, one of the last to be rescued, having led his platoon through enemy lines on a captured horse.

A few weeks later, he was posted to the Middle East. It was decided that my mother would take us to America to join up with our American cousins in Philadelphia. Uncle Tom, my father's brother, had already enlisted as a doctor to the British army. Linda always said the next three years there were some of the happiest times in her life. Unlike her, I have no memories of them. But I do remember the voyage back to England on an aircraft carrier in 1943. I was tied by a long rope to a fitting on the deck so that I would not fall overboard and fed with Hershey bars by kind American sailors.

When we got back to England, my mother went to live near our Camrose grandmother at Audley's Wood, where two of her sisters with their children were already installed. Linda and Thomas shared a governess there with their cousins Robin, Adrian and Philip while Christophe (aged 3) and I made mud-pies in the garden. Hackwood was still in use as a hospital for the Canadian army, with Nissan huts all over the lawn, and our parents' house in Kent was still a prime target for German bombs. When we returned there a year later, there were lots of exciting bomb craters cut into the chalk exposing the tangled roots of ancient beech and oak. Linda and I made houses there and in winter went for thrilling toboggan rides down Biggin Hill.

After the war, our father resolved to take up farming full-time. He bought sheep and pigs, kept horses and a few cows. There was a row of tumble-down cottages where the farm workers lived. Their children wore cut-down men's trousers and too large gumboots, but they were fun to play with and formed part of our gang. But my happiest memory of Kent were the cherry trees. There were two sorts of cherries, the red ones that stained your clothes and the pink and white ones, even more delicious, that did not. Linda and I shared a stolid Shetland pony which we could ride down an avenue of cherries, plucking bunches as we went. In term-time, we went to a local PNEU school by bus, with Linda aged 8 in charge. Petrol was strictly rationed and visits to neighbours were few – I dimly remember two children called Ward who lived in a grand house called Squerries which had black swans on a lake.

Nigel was born in the early autumn of 1946. When he

was imminent, Linda and I were packed off to stay with our McNair Scott grandparents in Surrey. Our grandmother was Swedish and easy to fool. We both detested fish and Linda firmly informed her that we were not allowed to eat it and she struggled valiantly to feed us from the meagre post-war rations of corned beef and spam. Our Scottish grandfather taught us to play spillikins with beautiful ivory spillikins from China. As a young man he had worked in the family business, Guthries, which owned huge rubber plantations in the Malay States. Now he and his wife lived contentedly in their pretty cottage with a large garden – the garden was full of rock-plants and delicious alpine strawberries.

Soon after Nigel's birth, my father bought a larger farm in Hampshire, within easy reach of our other grandparents at Hackwood Park. The new farm was called Huish, which meant a damp place in Anglo-Saxon, and lay in a dip between sloping chalk fields. There was a shallow lake planted with watercress, which a local farmer and his two sons cut daily in bunches to send to market, and a stream where Linda and I and Thomas could paddle about in army surplus rubber dinghies. My father had bought a herd of little black cows called Dexters (related to Irish Kerry cattle) with which he soon won prizes at the local agricultural shows. They gave rich milk, which my mother laboriously strained and churned to make butter. Butter was a luxury; 2 oz a week was the ration, and when you went out to tea, you took your butter with you.

Huish house itself was a perfect example of early 1900s 'Stockbroker Tudor', with mullioned windows, dark panelling and old oak beams. It had long corridors and masses of bedrooms and attics which were wonderful for hide-and-seek and a sunken garden perfect for Kick-the-Can. The landscape beyond was duller than the dramatic chalk downs of Kent which we had left. But there were woods filled with bluebells and yellow archangel and a network of rides along the edges of corn fields.

I was enrolled in a new PNEU school in Basingstoke, but Linda, now nearly eleven, was packed off to Southover Manor in Sussex. It was an odd choice by my parents, three hours' drive away from home, and a school that prided itself on being 'non-academic'. Girls left at 16 and were then expected to go to a finishing school in Switzerland or elsewhere and after a London season marry a suitable man. There was no provision for taking A-levels or going to university. But they had been seduced by the headmistress, Miss Aspden, a Moral Re-armer who preached the gospel of solid parenthood (no children of divorces were allowed) and meeting 'nice girls'. Linda later described her time there as encompassing 'acres of boredom' but she made friends easily, read endless novels and historical fiction, mainly Georgette Heyer and Margaret Irwin, and in the holidays brought her best friends to stay.

Three years later, I too was packed off to the same boarding school, and hated it. Everything depended on having best friends to sit next to at tea or to walk to church with; if not you had to walk with the teacher and were despised. Linda tried her best to comfort me and I would sob in her room every evening after tea. But in the end, I found a best friend, Tricia Knight (now Daunt), and all was well.

Back at home Hampshire was a hotbed of teenage social life. At least five or six times every holidays, we would be invited to children's dances in neighbouring country houses, inhabited by rich stockbrokers or local squires. (Years later I was fascinated to discover the same squires' names and houses in many of Jane Austen's letters.) Linda and I usually wore matching party dresses – cheap blue net over satin, made by the local dressmaker, who lived in a dark cottage in Old Basing. Off we would go, squashed into a taxi with our older brother Thomas, my spirits sinking at every mile we got nearer the dance. Sure enough, when we got there, Linda was whisked off to dance by admiring boys and I was left standing miserably against a wall. She did her best to help me – ordering her admirers to send their younger brothers to ask me to dance. The only bright spot was the Dashing White Sergeant in which trios set to each other – two boys with a girl between them or two girls with one boy. Linda would rush over to rescue me with her current swain. But sometimes, my only option was to retreat upstairs and hide in a bedroom until the longed-for taxi came at midnight to take us home.

Why was Linda so good at social life and I so hopeless? I never quite knew. In both cases, we had the example of a highly sociable father who could talk to anyone, and a mother who had literally NO small talk. I think Linda learnt early to make conversation because she had to; my older brother Thomas was as shy as I was and in the end refused to go to parties at all. Gillian was already married and only swam into view on rare occasions. In vain, Linda instructed me that all you had to do was to ask boys about themselves. It took me years to follow her advice.

The same pattern followed when it came to a so-called London season. Linda, by now equipped with ravishing ball dresses made by Belinda Bellville, 'came out' in 1954 and was an instant success. It is said that the leading bandsman, Tommy Kinsman, struck up her favourite Cole Porter song, 'Smoke Gets in Your Eyes', whenever she appeared on the dance floor. And there is a wonderful picture of her, which I think appeared in the *Tatler*, in a white tulle and lace dress, sitting on the steps of our grandfather's house in Carlton House Terrace, with her pretty retroussé nose in profile. (How I envied her nose – mine was large and bony like my father's.) She brought down dashing young men for weekends at Huish, who played racing demon with Nigel and me and brought us large boxes of chocolates. One of them, Dmitri Kasterine, even called later to take me out from boarding school. I described him boastfully to the other girls as a Russian Prince.

I only started to emerge from painful shyness when I was sent to school in Paris two years later. Paris was full of men rolling their eyes at me and asking hopefully, 'Vous êtes suédoise?' (I had blonde hair and Swedish girls were reputed easy lays.) Then, like Linda, I attended a finishing school called Cuffys in Oxford. Cuffy (real name Mlle Hubler) was Swiss and had come to England as governess to the Bonham Carters, Asquith's grandchildren, thirty years before. She was very plain but had eloped to everyone's surprise with Lady Violet Bonham Carter's lover, Foxy Falk, who had been a Cambridge Apostle and a great friend of Maynard Keynes and G. E. Moore. She set up house with him in Merton Street overlooking the Oxford Examination Halls, and would take six or seven girls at a time, teaching them about French literature. She also gave them a smattering of German and a veneer of culture by sending them (uninvited) to the best lectures in Oxford such as Lord David Cecil's on English literature or Professor Gombrich's on European art. It was she who inspired Linda for her future books on the French Romantic poets and French history in general.

Cuffy was also responsible for encouraging me to try for Oxford proper. It was the first time in my life I did not follow in Linda's footsteps. I took the exams in Cuffy's boudoir in the spring of 1957 and was accepted to read Modern Languages that autumn. Linda had chosen instead to go on to art school in London, partly because she was in love with someone who was working in the City, partly because she loved drawing, having been enthused by her teacher at Southover, Quentin Bell.

When I came back to London, three years later, Linda found us a ground floor flat in an ex-pub off the Fulham Road. Then I found a much nicer one in a modern block two streets away overlooking the garages of Chelsea square. It had a large sunny balcony from which we could watch the chauffeurs polishing up their owners' cars.

Linda was now working at *Vogue* as travel editor. She had been there five years and had worked her way up from writing fashion copy. Early in 1961, encouraged by Linda, I went in for the Vogue Talent contest and much to my surprise won. So I gave in my notice and, like Linda, now took the No 14 bus along the Fulham Road to Oxford Street every morning to work at Condé Nast in Hanover Square. There was a grand glass foyer with smart lifts to the second floor. The senior fashion editors would look you sternly up and down in the lift to check your appearance. Linda and I both usually wore Chanel-style suits bought from Wallis Shops in Oxford Street and pointed patent leather shoes from Saxone. Linda shared an office with the features editor, Mary Holland, who was her great friend. I was in the copywriters' pool in an open plan office, next to the editor. Linda was working much harder, commissioning articles of travel from famous writers or writing pieces about trips abroad taken by herself.

After two years in this cosy office, I was offered a job on the *Daily Mail* as Shirley Conran's assistant on her so-called Ideal Home Page. The new job came as a shock. Fleet Street took ages to get to – no more nice No 14 bus, and the *Daily Mail* was a bastion of male dominance.

Shirley Conran worked in a room with the two other women columnists and there was no desk space for me; I was installed at one belonging to the terrifying Anne Scott James, who only came in on occasions. I knew nothing of homemaking or even cooking – I had only ever cooked frozen peas and scrambled eggs. I became slightly less hopeless as time went on, but I hated the sunless office with no friends to gossip with, or eat lunch with. I would return to the flat in Fulham every evening to wail to Linda about my horrible day. In the end, she advised me to give notice, which I did – much to Shirley's relief.

By now, Linda had got engaged to Laurence. He exactly fitted what she had always wanted – intellectual, brilliant at languages, part outsider, yet also part of a circle of clever public-school friends who had all been at Oxford together. Before that her boyfriends had been either solid right-wing Etonians working in the City or bohemian slightly raffish left-wing journalists whom she had met through work. I was miserable at the thought of her leaving our flat, and found Laurence alarmingly bouncy and energetic. But after they married, she was only a bus ride away at the far end of the Fulham Road, where Laurence owned a little house, nominally a garage which had to be hastily reconverted to such if a housing inspector called. Linda had given up her job at *Vogue*, which she missed a lot, and now spent her time cooking delicious meals for Laurence, who had high standards inculcated by his Belgian mother, Lady Kelly, and giving dinner parties. I went to supper often and also to dinners with Lady Kelly who took a fancy to me and to my older sister Gillian, who lived round the corner from her. (She was not always so nice to Linda, partly because she was not Catholic, but mainly because Linda had removed Laurence from living under her roof.) At one of Lady Kelly's dinners, I caught the eye of Thomas, Laurence's close friend and best man. The rest, as they say, is history.

After six months in the 'garage', Linda and Laurence bought 44 Ladbroke Grove – then a huge dark barn of a house. I think it cost them £5,000. Notting Hill was only beginning to be fashionable; Henrietta (Thomas' cousin) and Willie Phipps were already living in Chepstow Villas and soon afterwards Vanessa and Hugh Thomas bought their house at the southern end of Ladbroke Grove.

By the time I got married to Thomas a year-and-a-half later, no. 44 had been transformed to the comfortable house it is now. Then Thomas and I went to live in Ireland – in a flat in Dublin which I hated, and Tullynally which I loved. We gave up the flat, but after a few years in the country, Thomas became restless and announced he would have to live partly in Dublin or London to be able to write books. I chose London – mainly to be near Linda and the rest of my family and friends. Linda found us a terrace house in Ladbroke Grove just beside Ladbroke Square, and a school for Maria, now aged 5. So now I was back near her, sharing the school runs, and our children played together in Ladbroke Square or Linda's communal garden. Then Fred was born and we moved to the larger house in Elgin Crescent also with a communal garden. Linda by now was busy writing books, and did not share my boredom and frustration at not having enough to do. In the end, I was offered the chance to write a book too – on the Edwardian empire – but found it agony to write. I would sit in the first-floor drawing room of our Elgin Crescent house arranging and rearranging card-indexes on the window seat, first at one end of the room, then at the other, or taking bicycle rides to the Portobello Road – anything to escape writing. Linda would telephone to give advice, 'Murder your darlings' she would say, as I complained of the difficulty of fitting in yet one more quotation from my index cards without losing the narrative thread. Without her, I do not think I would ever have written the book. After that, I embarked on the much easier task of putting together anthologies, or editing letters which only needed footnotes or short introductory captions. Unlike her, I have always hated proper writing.

After 25 years living part-time in London, our children had left school, and Thomas and I went back to live mainly in Ireland, and inevitably saw less of Linda. But she was always there at the end of a telephone or would come bustling down the hill to visit us in our small London house in Nottingdale. As always, she would cheer us up and provide us with sound advice. For us and for all her friends and family, Linda was a rock, an indestructible rock of unselfish love and affection.

*

A Brother's Memory by Nigel McNair Scott

Linda was brave, constant, pretty, clever and fun.

My first memory of her was on Christmas morning 1948 when she led Thomas and Valerie into the night nursery, her fair hair shining, laughing and shouting for pure joy. My next was her at the top of a very tall fir – she was good at climbing trees – on the Huish drive, triumphantly smiling down at a group of worried adults – a feat much to be emulated.

She was kind to a brother nine years her junior and used to read to me in the evenings till I fell asleep. One book was *The Princess and the Goblins* and I sometimes wonder whether the scene where Curdie leads the Princess through the underground tunnels with walls shining with ore inspired me to build gold mines.

The house was quiet when she and Valerie went to school, but when they came back it became full of her friends: the Makins twins – I named my rabbit after Mollie; the eldest Gilchrist girl; and Anne Louise Stockdale, all being sweet to her little brother. In the summer there were endless games of tennis and kick-the-can, and tea time, with its white cloths and plates of brown bread and butter with honey or jam, was full of girlish voices discussing books, and clothes and parties, no longer a silent dining room as our mama did not speak much and Thomas and I rarely uttered. The music seems to have been Burl Ives singing 'The Big Rock Candy Mountain'.

New friends arrived in the year she came out. The sun shone – much croquet was played and I picture her now lying on the chaise longue in the garden in a broad-brimmed white hat laughing up at her admirers. In the background *Salad Days* was playing on the new gramophone and at least one of her swains was quite good at ping pong.

Later came art school and *Vogue*. She was a not inconsiderable artist – I still have two charming small oils – and was excellent at sketching ladies' dresses. She also transformed Huish by persuading my parents to pickle and lime the dark oak panelling in the dining room and sitting room and redecorating one of the bathrooms with exotic pheasants copied from the Chinese room at Hackwood.

We became quite close after she and I were both ill in 1959 and our parents took us one grey spring week to convalesce in the Imperial Hotel in Torquay where there was little to do but sit in the ballroom listening to the band playing tea-time melodies. On the subject of tea, thereafter she would come and take me out for it at Eton where she looked so young and pretty I hoped people would think she was my girlfriend.

I remember her first small house with Laurence with an enormous bed and then the excitement of seeing the great empty shell of Ladbroke Grove before they decided in a pioneering way to buy it but most of all how it became filled with her friends. One of them from art school – Alyson Glover – married James Spooner who took me on as his personal assistant because of Linda. When he left to become a partner at Rothschilds he placed me with two other friends of Linda's in a mining house.

At that time James was chairman of Helical Bar, a small struggling rebar merchant that Laurence and his friend Dick Hill took on. Years later this led to Laurence's deal with Mike Slade and the replenishment of our family's fortunes much depleted by school fees and our father's later investment policies.

My job with James was the first of many kindnesses I received from being Linda's brother. Even now I meet people who remember her coming out, at art school and at a myriad of other places, and I bathe in reflected glory.

I could go on: searching out Notting Hill houses, the elegance of *Vogue's* offices, her flat in Dovehouse Street, climbing into Ladbroke Grove by a drain pipe after dances, and the endless discussions yet again at her feet on the chaise longue in the drawing room covering family, children, grandchildren, cousinage which she believed in – she wrote most of my eulogy about Adrian – detective novels, pictures and places.

Most of all, I remember her heroic determination not to give way to self-pity, and her love and her faith to preserve and enhance Laurence's life through so many years of illness while also caring so lovingly for her children and their offspring.

I miss her very much.

A Hampshire Childhood by Hermione Moncreiffe

I first knew Linda when I was six and she was seven. We lived near each other in Hampshire during the War in 1943. Linda's family lived at Huish House near Basingstoke and we were in my aunt 's house at Dummer village. We did morning lessons together, which were organised by Linda's mother's clever sister Sheila Birkenhead, one of Lord and Lady Camrose's huge family, with an excellent governess, Miss Dwire. Before Linda arrived in the class, it was held at Hackwood, the Camrose's house, but then moved to the Birkenhead's house, Audley's Wood. The pupils were the Birkenhead's son Robin Furneaux, another cousin of Linda's, Philip Chetwode, and a few others, children of neighbours.

We learnt a great deal of poetry. I remember Robin reciting Blake's 'Tiger, Tiger, burning bright' with great vigour, and Philip reciting Tennyson's, 'The Brook'. I learnt the sad Keats poem, 'I had a dove and the sweet dove died'. Linda had no problem with learning poetry such as, 'O young Lochinvar is come out of the west', and many more. I wish I had a clearer memory of her, but I do remember her and me singing together, 'Au Clair de la Lune'. The only literary endeavour that I can remember was John M. Floyd's 'At Xmas for Dinner we had Hen'.

Sheila did the most imaginative thing of taking some of us to see a production in London of *Richard III*, which once I got over the first feeling of incomprehension I found absolutely thrilling and can still remember bits of. I thought the reason I was taken to the play was that my mother knew the Duke of Gloucester. Another memory I have of Sheila is of her taking us to a grassy stage, like a sort of little hill in a wood, and getting us to recite.

In these days I particularly liked Linda and remember her as being very competent and somehow more grown-up than the rest of us. She was certainly better at doing everything than I was. Also, she was very pretty with her very fair hair.

Linda's mother (Mary), Mrs McNair Scott, was exceptionally good with small children and I have never forgotten a wonderful party she gave at their home Huish House. She managed to make even the shyest child like me feel totally relaxed. At some stage at the party she put all the lights out, how exciting it all was.

Sometimes Linda's grandparents, the Camroses, had a children's film show at Hackwood, showing such films as Walt Disney's *Bambi*.

The other neighbours who gave children's parties were the Portsmouths at Farley Wallop. These tea parties had really delicious food, particularly appreciated in these bleak times of the War. Later our lessons were moved to Farley Wallop and joined by Phillipa Wallop with occasional visits by Jane, too young to fully join the class.

We moved to live near Winchester when I was eight, and then up to Scotland and I didn't see Linda again until she was seventeen.

'Lochinvar', by Sir Walter Scott

O young Lochinvar is come out of the west,
Through all the wide Border his steed was the best;
And save his good broadsword he weapons had none,
He rode all unarm'd, and he rode all alone.
So faithful in love, and so dauntless in war,
There never was knight like the young Lochinvar.

He staid not for brake, and he stopp'd not for stone,
He swam the Eske river where ford there was none;
But ere he alighted at Netherby gate,
The bride had consented, the gallant came late:
For a laggard in love, and a dastard in war,
Was to wed the fair Ellen of brave Lochinvar.

So boldly he enter'd the Netherby Hall,
Among bride's-men, and kinsmen, and brothers and all:
Then spoke the bride's father, his hand on his sword,
(For the poor craven bridegroom said never a word,)
'O come ye in peace here, or come ye in war,
Or to dance at our bridal, young Lord Lochinvar?'

'I long woo'd your daughter, my suit you denied;—
Love swells like the Solway, but ebbs like its tide—
And now I am come, with this lost love of mine,
To lead but one measure, drink one cup of wine.
There are maidens in Scotland more lovely by far,
That would gladly be bride to the young Lochinvar.'

The bride kiss'd the goblet: the knight took it up,
He quaff'd off the wine, and he threw down the cup.
She look'd down to blush, and she look'd up to sigh,
With a smile on her lips and a tear in her eye.
He took her soft hand, ere her mother could bar,—
'Now tread we a measure!' said young Lochinvar.

So stately his form, and so lovely her face,
That never a hall such a galliard did grace;
While her mother did fret, and her father did fume,
And the bridegroom stood dangling his bonnet and plume;
And the bride-maidens whisper'd, ''twere better by far
To have match'd our fair cousin with young Lochinvar.'

One touch to her hand, and one word in her ear,
When they reach'd the hall-door, and the charger stood near;

So light to the croupe the fair lady he swung,
So light to the saddle before her he sprung!
'She is won! we are gone, over bank, bush, and scaur;
They'll have fleet steeds that follow,' quoth young Lochinvar.

There was mounting 'mong Graemes of the Netherby clan;
Forsters, Fenwicks, and Musgraves, they rode and they ran:
There was racing and chasing on Cannobie Lee,
But the lost bride of Netherby ne'er did they see.
So daring in love, and so dauntless in war,
Have ye e'er heard of gallant like young Lochinvar?

*

My memories of Linda by Harriet Cullen

Something which stuck in my mind always was Laurence's saying, more than once, that the secret of a happy marriage was never quite knowing or understanding the other person. He had chosen wisely in this. I have hesitated quite a few weeks trying to put down on paper what I felt and remembered best of my cousin Linda, and what it was that I loved and what made her really tick. There was something deeply unfathomable and mysterious about her; she was a person of many layers.

She was nine years older than me, the third child of my father's older sister Mary, and I only got to know her as a teenager, perhaps first at a hunt ball in their house near Basingstoke, where she and her sister Valerie dazzled me, both blonde beauties with egg-timer figures shimmering in black, watched proudly by the Master, their charming and glamorous father Ronnie. Another early meeting I think was a summer gathering of first cousins hosted by our genial widowed grandmother Camrose (Moggie) in the munificent surroundings of Gleneagles Hotel outside

Perth. Linda seemed fun and serene and it was only some years later that I learnt that she resented our grandmother. Moggie had been a hard mother to Linda's mother, the first born, who had suffered the tensions of the rapidly rising and expanding Berry family. It's possible that some of that tension passed down to Linda and helped form a sliver of flint at the heart of her sweet and giving nature. Certainly, to put it simply, she combined some Welsh flint from her matter-of-fact, shy and highly intelligent mother, with the grace and vitality and silver tongue of her father and his Scottish and Swedish forebears.

I started to see Linda more when I came to live in London, when she had recently married Laurence and they had set up house in Ladbroke Grove – an adventurous purchase in a still rough area. It was a large Victorian villa, made comfortable and elegant with Laurence's family pictures, and William Morris carpets and chaise longue – on which, memorably, a woman guest once stripped – 'Don't stop, Camilla,' cried the silver-tongued hostess, 'you look so pretty!' For the cousinage, it became a wonderful hub for interesting talk and gossip, more bohemian (despite Linda's neat conservative clothes) and cosy than the old-style '60s London salons. (Although Linda said ruefully, 'We went through that five year period of just having to weed out a lot of each other's old friends…')

Given her intelligence, it seemed extraordinary that she had left school at sixteen. She was unnecessarily modest about her painting studies at Byam Shaw – I used to hear more about her years on *Vogue*, where she became travel editor with her own secretary by the age of twenty and had to defend her professional dignity at the office from Laurence appearing in a Tom Wolfe suit waving a rose at her. Unobtrusively, she was very widely read, in French as well as English, in early detective stories as well as most

European classics, and had a swift power of recall. As for her literary career – ten biographies of Romantic and Regency figures and their circles – it seems like magic sleight of hand to have combined it throughout with caring for her family, which never became less onerous. Maybe it was grace held up by sinewy determination, and a policy not to see the downside, for which some friends teased her as Dr Pangloss, and yet she had to face it in her darker hours. She would say, 'It's no use worrying if you just can't do anything about it'; although she did do a great deal about it.

It's a cliché to say that her books were fine-spun, but I was watching over her shoulder once on a train coming back from Cumbria; she was sitting in a group of us ignoring the criss-cross of chat, and fiddling with her pencil, patiently, on a long complex paragraph. It really did seem like spinning, which I have seen in the Andean high plateau.

When I married Martín she welcomed him into her side of the family, feeling a new kinship for her young cousin who had also chosen outside the Anglo-Saxon box, and I think she loved her long talks with him on life and books and writing. Her visit with Laurence to Argentina and to Martín's estancia was a sort of culmination of this.

When I became involved with the Keats-Shelley House and its charity Linda helped generously, introducing me to her own much more high-powered literary friends, among others to the Wordsworth Trust group in Grasmere. She never failed, almost to the last, to come and give moral support at the annual Keats-Shelley Prize which I ran. Once she hosted a party for this at Ladbroke Grove. It started off decorous and dignified and ended riotously. A young girlfriend of Lucien Freud returned home to collapse over his feet, murmuring *KeatshhShhelley*... a brilliant bit of cross-fertilisation of the arts brought about by Linda. Another even more generous act of hosting was for my sister Eleanor, when her boyfriend died. Linda and Laurence had been so kind so often to them both. Now Linda was already ill but wearing it lightly, and insisted on organising the wake at her house, a short distance from the funeral at Kensal Rise.

I still haven't got to the bottom of how she ticked.

*

Lunch with Linda by Mollie Norwich

Linda and I lunched together for nearly seventy years. Our parents were neighbours, we went to the same boarding school, we shared a flat in London in the 1950s and were the best of friends. We had lunches as children, lunches with children, holiday lunches, proper lunches at Ladbroke Grove with stimulating and amusing guests, and most recently usually settled for lunch *à deux* in an Italian restaurant in Notting Hill. There the set menu remained reassuringly unchanged: our particular favourite was *vitello al limone* with superb mashed potatoes preceded by *bruschetta al pomodoro*. Sometimes we had a glass of wine, sometimes not. Soon we hardly bothered to order, the charming owner just needed a nod and the food arrived.

And we talked and talked. There was never a dearth of subjects. What we had been doing, whom we had seen, where we had been. Some enjoyable gossip, though Linda was totally discreet and one of the few people I have known who would *never* pass on a confidence. She could also be counted on for very wise advice for any dilemma.

Our most enduring topic was books. What we had been reading (and in Linda's case, writing or researching), suggestions for re-reading and discussions about past favourites. She had a passion for detective stories and thrillers but was *very* particular about which ones to read. She adored Dick Francis and re-read him constantly. She introduced me to Martin Walker and his Dordogne detective and to Philip Kerr's policeman in Nazi Germany. We usually gave each other a book for Christmas and Linda recommended the excellent wheeze of reading the intended gift before passing it on. Her presents, often by authors I had never heard of, were always winners. From experience I, on the other hand, swiftly learned to ask her exactly which book she wanted – often they were on entirely unexpected or obscure subjects in which she had become interested and which I in turn enjoyed. One such was the group biography of the young optimists who kick-started the Industrial Revolution, *The Lunar Men*.

Linda also encouraged re-visiting some of our childhood favourites, in particular Georgette Heyer's novels, which she admired, with her historian's sensibility, for the authenticity of the language and Regency background as well as their seductive narratives.

When younger, we had shared a dream of working in a bookshop. Most of the time was to be spent reading at the till while occasionally giving advice to a customer or perhaps even selling the occasional book. So I was thrilled when she suggested at lunch one day that we should take a joint share in a venture being started by James Daunt, the son of great friends, so as to belatedly fulfil part of that fantasy. After a shaky start, the shop in Marylebone High Street proved a great success – partly due to Linda's gentle nudging of her many literary friends that they should hold their launch parties there, a tradition to this day. We were bought out as the business expanded, but Linda was thrilled when a branch opened close to her home in Notting Hill. She had an extremely good financial brain and this was one of several suggested investments. Most I considered too risky though often, to my chagrin, they turned out extremely well.

We used to bewail the fact that we had been sent to such a hopeless boarding school by our parents and the subsequent lack of a university education. But, in Linda's case, that scarcely mattered. She became travel editor of *Vogue*, published ten acclaimed and beautifully written 18th century histories, and was a superb letter writer. She had a wonderful memory for poetry and light verse, and she and my husband John Julius would exchange their discoveries with glee. A particular favourite was *The Ballad of Mrs Ravoon* where each would write new verses to send to the other by postcard. She was also a regular and inspired source of material for his annual *Christmas Crackers*.

Oh, how I miss our lunches…

*

Making the Best of Life by Prue Mosselmans

When we were 30 Linda said we should start using face cream. I ought, as always, to have taken her advice.

I think we became friends at our appalling school because we both read every book in the library, and at our several thousand lunches at The Portico over 60 years we mostly talked about books. She took my son Fred to Murder One (the famous Charing Cross bookshop specialising in crime fiction) when he was about 10 and he has been hooked on detective stories ever since.

At 19 we spent three months in Rome studying art. Linda became friends with Nicola Pietrangeli (the legendary Italian tennis player) and we spent many hours watching tennis. One lunch we decided to order just cream (usually they ate cream with fraises des bois) – a disastrous idea. We both fell in love with Villa Giulia.

During the heatwave of 2003 we were alone in London. It was much too hot to visit so we spent hours on the telephone instead.

Like Burns's friend, Linda made the best of life. It is tough without her.

'Epitaph On A Friend' by Robert Burns

> An honest man here lies at rest,
> The friend of man, the friend of truth,
> The friend of age, and guide of youth:
> Few hearts like his, with virtue warm'd,
> Few heads with knowledge so inform'd:
> If there's another world, he lives in bliss;
> If there is none, he made the best of this.

*

Birds of Passage by Nina Lobanov-Rostovsky

When we moved to London from San Francisco in August 1979, Nikita contacted all his Oxford friends. Linda and Laurence immediately asked us to tea at 44 Ladbroke Grove. It was the first of many visits to their hospitable home.

While Nikita and Laurence caught up with each other, partly in English and partly in Russian – for Laurence likes to practice his fluent Russian with Nikita – Linda and I chatted. One of the first things she asked me was: 'Are you going to be birds of passage or are you settling in London?' Slightly surprised by the question, I replied that I hoped we would be here for many years, for after a diplomatic childhood with numerous moves I didn't like changing homes and countries though I did enjoy travelling. Linda then told me how happy she was that Laurence hadn't become a diplomat like his father for she would have hated moving from one country to another, making friends, then having to leave then behind. 'I find it painful enough to make friends with foreign diplomats in London who then leave, taking a bit of my heart with them.'

*

My Aunt Linda by Crispin Kelly

'À chaque jour suffit sa peine.'

We had the relationship of nephew and aunt. This meant that I could eat lunch often at Ladbroke Grove without feeling too bad about how rarely I returned the hospitality. After all, I had to raise my level of conversation to the intellectual.

In this, I am reminded of lunches with Linda's mother-in-law, Marie-Noelle. She too presided over a table where discussion and an exchange of ideas was the main dish. I have come to feel that Linda's relationship with Marie-Noelle and the aura of Frenchness about her particularly delighted her. She was intrigued and increasingly taken up in our extensive French and Belgian cousinhood. She knew them all, embraced them and their multiplying generations.

This seemed to chime with her professional life, often taken up with French subjects. This delight in Frenchness seemed to marry with her natural elegance. She did after all have a dog called Duchess, fine of bone and luxurious of coat. This elegance segued naturally into an appetite for conversation. French was of course the language of diplomacy, as exemplified by Marie-Noelle, the ambassador's wife. Linda had the outstanding ability to summon the right aphorism to mark the end of any conversational subject. In the last year, 'À chaque jour suffit sa peine' was one that came to the fore, making me realise the more how bravery and stoicism lay behind the elegance.

In the stillness of the drawing room at number 44, I wondered at her treasure trove of apothegms. They were sparkling delights, optimistic, knowing and encouraging. I knew of another corner of her appetites, which was her love of a good detective story. They seemed to share something of the quality of an aphorism: self-contained, economic and knowing. She was herself reluctant to embark on writing one, as she felt she didn't have a good enough plot to hand. In recent years I liked to dig out more obscure who-dunnits to entertain her. Recently in New York I got some very left-field examples for her: native American cops, Alaskan sleuths…but wasn't entirely surprised that she knew them already. These tales were good places to contain and quarantine bad things.

Getting back onto my Vespa after lunch with her, I always knew I had been well fed.

*

Two Newly-weds in a Sportscar by Thomas Williams

I was a page at Linda and Laurence's wedding, she as radiant and lovely as always. One of my earliest memories was a visit to their new house, 44 Ladbroke Grove. Since, in those days, the place was considered to be on the furthest fringes of the civilised world, they led us in a convoy. Laurence was in a rather snappy, two-seater sports car, so that we children following could only watch in dismay as the two newly-weds sped away into the distance – a metaphor, no doubt, for Linda's brilliant future career.

I believe she had followed Gillian, my mother, her older sister, to art school before working for *Vogue*. At Huish there was a charming bathroom painted by her, showing peacocks, birds and flowering trees, always a place of wonder for me as a child. After she married, she quickly accumulated an encyclopaedic knowledge of literature and history, of which some areas – such as English Romanticism and the French cultural diaspora in the early 19th century – were to become her personal fiefdoms. Her books were models of construction, so logical and well thought-out that she could use a simple, unpretentious style of writing that we must all hope to emulate. She was always willing to share her vast and accurate fund of learning without hesitation or condescension.

***

A Guiding Spirit to Others

Consolations by Rachel Kelly

My earliest memory of my mother as a writer was her making cups of coffee. This she would do throughout her working day. She always said she struggled to get down to work and making coffee was a displacement activity. I think, though, she loved the writing life, and always instilled in us children the importance of work. But if she had to choose, we her family always came first.

Coffee came a close second. I can see her waiting for the kettle to boil in the kitchen. She liked Nescafé Gold

Blend and regular milk. The cup was always of china, not pottery, as she said coffee tasted better drunk from porcelain. She had a fondness for white china cups covered in roses or wild flowers.

Now I see her walking up the stairs at Ladbroke Grove, coffee mug in hand. And now at her desk, surrounded by discarded cups which made brown circles on the A4 sheets of typing paper in her top floor eyrie.

Though I studied History at university, on the whole our literary interests did not overlap. She was a historian and lover of the 18th-century. I chose to write about mental health and wellbeing, including a memoir called *Black Rainbow* about my own experience of two severe depressive episodes.

But there was one literary overlap between us: poetry. I always had loved poetry and so did she. When I was growing up, if something went wrong, my mother had the poem for it.

When I had my heart broken as a teenager, she gave me 'Apple Blossom' by Louis MacNeice, with its line 'The first blossom was the best blossom/For the child who had never seen an orchard.' There would be other blossoms; other love affairs. Now I wish I had asked her more about her own heart-broken moments, but I doubt she would have told me.

She was discreet. While not prudish, she didn't wish to dwell on her subjects' physical passions. In her work she was naturally drawn to the introspection and sensibility of the Romantic era – in her studies of Chatterton, Tom Moore, and her 'Young Romantics' – rather than the licentiousness and confident, if not brash, outward show of the earlier Restoration and Augustan periods.

It was not that she did not feel deeply. She did. But her curiosity was for what German romantics, borrowing from Latin, called 'Individuum': the individual's mind, body and spirit, in all its complexity. I grew up with a sense that she believed in joy, yes, but she was realistic about the poignancy of unfulfilled hopes and dreams too, rather than any fairytale fantasy view of life. She was drawn to poetry and literature which evoked a delicate *not knowing*, poems of exploration, interior discovery and ambiguity which she shared with me.

I followed her example. Throughout my 20s and early 30s, whenever a friend needed comfort, I would send a poem that had helped me. Some joked that I ran a sort of poetry pharmacy, prescribing words instead of pills.

Then I fell ill with depression. Now, in sickness, I was the one in need of poetic consolation, and my mother was a rich source. She knew literally hundreds of poems off by heart. She joked that she knew so many poems because there had been nothing else to do at Southover, her boarding school. Actually, she had an astonishing memory and a profound love of poetic language.

Her richly stocked mind came to my rescue when I was lying ill with serious depression. I was a child again, lying in bed as she read to me. It turned out that all these years she had been keeping a book of snippets of poetry, prayer and anecdotes that had particularly struck her.

I drank up the collection as if it were ice-cool water offered to a parched traveller. Indeed, I was so enthusiastic about her commonplace book that towards the end of her life I feel I can claim a tiny bit of credit for the fact that she decided to publish it. She wrote in the introduction of her *Consolations: a Commonplace book*: 'The collection has always been for my own consumption but recently I lent it to one of my daughters who was suffering from depression and she found it so comforting that I thought it might be a source of consolation – or interest or amusement for others too.'

Initially, I wasn't well enough to listen to, let alone read, anything longer than a few verses. Even that could exhaust me. I didn't have the attention span to read an entire novel. So poetry's brevity was a blessing. So too was the way it dissolved the feeling of solitude: I wasn't alone, as Mummy read to me. Others had suffered and made something of their suffering. They had reordered the seemingly random cruelty of the illness into some kind of sense.

Poetry absorbed and revitalised me. Its condensed nature and sophisticated vocabulary required a concentration that shocked me into the moment in an almost physical way, freeing me from worries past and future.

My mother and I began with short poems, many of which are dotted through the text of *Black Rainbow*. One favourite was *New Every Morning* by Susan Coolidge. It particularly helped at the painful start of the day:

> Every day is a fresh beginning,
> Listen my soul to the glad refrain.
> And, spite of old sorrows
> And older sinning,
> Troubles forecasted and possible pain,
> Take heart with the day and begin again.

Another favourite was the lyrics to Oscar Hammerstein's song 'You'll Never Walk Alone', which my mother would repeat as she held my hand. Later, as my concentration improved, I turned to the 17th century poet George Herbert, also a favourite of my mother's. When she read the first verse of 'Love (III)', I felt a bolt of electricity pierce through me. All the hairs on my arm stood on end.

> Love bade me welcome; yet my soul drew back,
> Guilty of dust and s*in*

The idea that my soul was 'guilty of dust and sin' seemed the most perfect description of depressive illness. The poem pinpointed a sense of guilt that I should be depressed even though I was blessed with a loving home, husband and children, feelings of shame that I had not previously acknowledged. Yet love wins through. My mother chose the poem for her funeral, and I recited it that day at St Mary of the Angels. It is the only poem I know so well I can recite it without a smidgen of worry that I could ever forget a line or verse.

We would also repeat phrases from 'The Flower' together, another Herbert poem. One of our favourites was 'Grief melts away/like snow in May'.

Later when I recovered, I edited a children's poetry anthology, dedicating it to my mother who has first instilled a love of poetry in me. I'm very fond of coffee too.

*

Linda and the Ladbroke Intelligentsia by Tom Stacey

Well, we wouldn't dream of rivalling the Bloomsbury Set, yet we could field a team, we of the Ladbroke Intelligentsia. We weren't Bloomsbury because we lacked the self-regarding conceit. Yet we packed in the creative talent with the minimum of showing off whether we wrote or painted or made bronzes or film or music, and we sort of circled and buzzed in the rarefied air at the top of Ladbroke Grove from Holland Park that centred upon number 44, across the road from St John's where composer-pianist Peter Roper-Curzon long mastered the music.

The past is my tense, though a recent past and only past at all because we've lost beloved Linda and one or two other luminaries whose glow, like hers, remains. Ladbroke's radius reaches a short step beyond the hill where Danish patriarch Canute ruled his brood – [C]Nut's family pluralising with a Norse *ing*, to give the hill its Notting name – south towards W8 and east into W2.

Ladbroke, W11, with its tree-girt grove brings up prime names I shall drop first: the Kellys, the Thomases, the Sampsons, and Stirlings... and straying just beyond: Pakenhams and Frasers, and eastwards Arnanders, with Byam-Shaws, Brunners and Taylors, as we stroll.

Dinner tables and cocktail parties, book launches and art exhibitions and chamber recitals mingled us. We Staceys came to play a part on Kensington Church Street. But Linda was the queen bee and her own family the inner hive, she with her pen's enthralling literary flow on eclectic topics, immaculately researched, exquisitely told. Her last anthology, *Consolations*, shows the reach of her private self. And regard her offspring: Rosanna, balletomane, translating from the Russian, wed to novelist and poet Anthony Gardner; and Rachel across the road with her family of Griggs, taking us out of darkness to good cheer in a series of curative books.

Meanwhile at home Linda's gifted spouse Laurence Kelly had given us *literati* two key biographies: first of Lermontov, Russia's poet-painter, and – defying a disabling stroke – of Griboyedov, the Russian playwright-diplomat, plus three historical anthologies on Istanbul, St Petersburg and Moscow, Laurence himself being briefly Moscow-reared, as son of Britain's ambassador to the Soviet Union when Stalin was tightening his stranglehold on Eastern Europe.

I first met Laurence as a fellow entrepreneur in Jeddah

where he was into steel and I into publishing. Hosting us there was none other than Christopher Arnander, Anglo-Swedish banker-musician, quietly brewing scholarly books on the Great War period, and his wife Primrose, who was putting together her enchanting series of Arabic adages with their English equivalents, and soon her biography of Gertrude Jekyll, her gardening ancestress. Soon they were to be ensconced at Hereford Road, W2.

Next along Ladbroke Grove was the family of Angus Stirling, Director-General of the National Trust, then Chairman of the Royal Opera House, all the while being a painter of high talent. And there, across the road, none but Hugh Thomas, the historian of Spain, married to Vanessa Jebb, gifted painter.

A bit further along Ladbroke Grove was Anthony Sampson, founding editor of South Africa's *Drum* magazine, later to lay out the entrails of power with his *Anatomy of Britain* and latterly to write the definitive biography of Nelson Mandela. A handful of winters ago Anthony was to leave us, and his popular widow, Sally, mourning.

Across the road from Ladbroke's southern entrance rises Campden Hill Square where Antonia Fraser *aka* Pinter presides amid the tribe of Pakenhams and Frasers, variously in our orbit... brother Thomas, chronicler of the scramble for Africa, and Antonia's banker son Benjie Fraser, poet of the City. All, surely, of Linda's broadly Ladbroke ambit.

And as for publishers to the Ladbroke's intelligentsia, I guess the favourite has been Chip Martin and his Starhaven imprint, launching each well-chosen title at Daunt's on Holland Park Avenue. Yet I, in modesty, confess a publishing part with my *Capuchin Classics* series, launched in 2008 from our neighbouring Clementi House, on the back of my international book publishing operation (cover for my own calling as novelist, Africanist and teller of long-short stories). As to the Capuchin imprint of over hundred titles warranting a new readership, Linda was to be inspirational for her flow of recommendations of both authors and introducers. Who was it but Linda bringing to the yeasty table of invigorating Capuchin lunches we hosted here among my wife Caroline Stacey's masterworks in bronze, the persons and ideas of – I snatch the names – Margaret Drabble, Kirsty Gunn, William Boyd, Ladbroke local Emma Tennant and a clutch more we honour.

Linda of the arrow judgment, of the literary sweep, the creative authority, the sparkle of her presence, queening the Ladbroke Intelligentsia.

*

Tom Moore at Bowood, 2012 by Oliver Williams

I have so many happy memories of Linda – of her taking us as children to the theatre, of lunch parties at Ladbroke Grove, of her company at family get-togethers. I remember her many kindnesses to me, well over and above any call of duty as my aunt and godmother, and her constant encouragement and support of my musical career.

As a nephew, I felt immensely proud when her first book appeared – *The Marvellous Boy*, a life of the poet Chatterton. Without claiming to have read her entire oeuvre, I have loved her books, my personal favourites being *The Young Romantics* and *Susanna, The Captain and the Castrato*, both written in that format, very much her own, where she interlinks several life stories. The latter, centred around the relationship between the Burney family and the singer Gasparo Pacchierotti, is an especially engaging read, like the best sort of novel. Sheridan once wrote that 'easy writing makes vile hard reading'. One only has to reverse that sentence. Of all historians Linda was easiest to read, the result, I am sure, of much 'vile hard' writing!

Her biography of Tom Moore, *Ireland's Minstrel*, came out in 2007. Moore, a prolific poet and friend of Byron's, is best known today for his 'Irish Melodies', setting words to ancient Irish airs, and to a lesser extent for his 'National Airs', setting words to tunes from other countries. I was thrilled when Linda asked me to accompany tenor Jeremy O'Sullivan and the Greek soprano Elena Marangou in a series of concerts celebrating Moore's life.

I have kept the programme for the fourth of these concerts, given in the splendid private chapel of Bowood House, and remember the event well. Linda introduced the concert with a short summary of Moore's life. Typically she had written three drafts of this before being finally satisfied! Then it was the turn of the music. As with any musical recital, I found that some parts flowed more easily than others. I struggled, I confess, with Benjamin Britten's arrangements of 'The Echo' and 'The Last Rose of Summer', or with what one perceptive member of the audience called Britten's 'wrong notes'. Settings of 'The Harmony of Music', 'Give Me the Harp of Epic Song' and 'Listen to the Muse's Lyre' by modern composer Tassis Christoyannis, were a delight with their folky Greek idiom and dance-rhythms; on the other hand they contained some rather scary changes of tempo, and on occasions Elena and I almost came adrift. There was no such problem with the arrangements by Moore's musical collaborator John Stevenson. These were a pleasure to play in their light Mendelssohnian style, and brilliantly sung by Jeremy. The pick of these was perhaps 'Believe Me, if All Those Endearing Young Charms', which tells of the lasting power of true love. Elena sang exquisitely in 'Dear Harp of my Country', this time arranged by Stanford. For me the highlights of the evening were the 'Two Venetian Songs', with music by Schumann from Moore's words translated to German. With Elena's singing and Schumann at his most lyrical, this was Heaven!

Linda and Laurence were kindness itself throughout the weekend, putting me up for the night at Ladbroke Grove on the eve of the concert. Linda even booked a minibus so that she, Laurence, Elena and I could travel from London to Bowood in comfort – a typically thoughtful gesture. How I miss her.

> Dear Harp of my country! in darkness I found thee,
> The cold chains of silence had hung o'er thee long,
> When proudly, my own island harp I unbound thee,
> And gave all thy chords to light, freedom and song.

– Opening lines of Moore's farewell to the *Irish Melodies*.

*

Acts of Kindness by Anthony Gardner

When my first collection of poems was published, I asked Linda if I might dedicate it to her. The wording I had in mind was 'For Linda Kelly, éminence grise'. But she said that she would prefer to do without the description – which, of course, only went to prove the point.

As a writer, she was extraordinarily productive. While other authors made a song and dance about their work in progress, she would quietly get on with it, like a swan whose feet propelled her invisibly beneath the surface, completing another book before you knew it. This was all the more remarkable because she put so much time and energy into advancing other people's interests.

Some of her selfless industry was in the public eye, as a trustee of the London Library and the Wordsworth Trust. But more often it took the form of acts of kindness known only to a small circle, such as lending the drawing-room of 44 Ladbroke Grove for a poetry reading or a book launch. Friends and relatives came to rely on her for editorial advice – which she gave without expectation of reward – and she delighted in making helpful introductions. If not for her, I would probably never have found my first publisher, to whom she sent – without telling me – a novel I'd given her to read; and when, after editing the Royal Society of Literature's magazine for a dozen years, I fell victim to an unexpected putsch, she rallied a great array of distinguished Fellows to take my part. Financially, too, she was generous and astute: she took particular pride in having backed her godson James Daunt's first bookshop.

All this is to speak only of the kindness she showed in the world of literature. But that, of course, was the world she loved best. I can hear her now, quoting with relish the words of Logan Pearsall Smith: 'People say that Life is the thing – but I prefer reading.'

*

No act of kindness, however small, is ever in vain.
— Aesop, 'The Lion and the Mouse'

Chosen by my mother as a contribution for her friend Hermione Moncreiffe's book of quotations, A Gathering of Honey: Inspiration from Mystics, Philosophers and Poets.

Flowers, painted by Linda as a young art student

Acknowledgements

I have a great many people to thank for their help while I was editing this book. First, I am extremely grateful to Mollie Norwich and Antonia Fraser for setting the wheels in motion by suggesting that my mother should be commemorated as a writer.

I would like to express gratitude to Valerie Pakenham for encouraging the project from the start, for reading work in progress and making valuable edits. I am also grateful to Thomas Pakenham for allowing me to use his wide-ranging address at my mother's funeral and his Christmas acrostic for her. I must thank Stoddard Martin for encouragement and for providing his review of my mother's last biography, which inspired my selection of scenes from her books. Christopher Sinclair-Stevenson gave help and advice. My father Laurence Kelly, my siblings Rachel and Nicky, and my uncle Nigel McNair Scott have all given unfailing encouragement.

I am particularly grateful to the many contributors who have been so generous in finding time to write about Linda: Marina Camrose, Harriet Cullen, Grey Gowrie, Anthony Gardner, Crispin Kelly, Rachel Kelly, Nina Lobanov-Rostovsky, Nigel McNair Scott, Hermione Moncreiffe, Prue Mosselmans, Mollie Norwich, Roland Philipps, David Pryce-Jones, Tom Stacey, Oliver Williams, Thomas Williams, Pamela Woof. I would also like to thank Patricia Rawlings for her support, Claire Weatherhead at Bloomsbury, Helen Atkinson for her copy-editing, and Ilona Phillips, who digitilised the illustrations.

Finally, I would like to thank my son Sasha Reviakin for his encouragement and patient technical backup, and my husband Anthony Gardner for his brilliant editorial guidance and constant support.

Books by Linda

The Marvellous Boy: The Life and Myth of Thomas Chatterton. Weidenfeld and Nicolson 1971; Faber Finds, 2009

The Young Romantics: Writers and Liaisons, Paris 1827-37. The Bodley Head, 1976; Starhaven (revised), 2003

The Kemble Era: John Philip Kemble, Sarah Siddons and the London Stage. Bodley Head, Random House (US), 1980

Women of the French Revolution. Hamish Hamilton, 1987; Penguin Books (paperback edition), 1989

Juniper Hall: An English Refuge from the French Revolution. Weidenfeld and Nicolson, 1991; Faber Finds, 2009

Richard Brinsley Sheridan: A Life. Sinclair-Stevenson, Random House, 1997

Susanna, the Captain and the Castrato: Scenes from the Burney Salon, 1779-80. Starhaven, 2004

Ireland's Minstrel: A Life of Tom Moore. I. B. Tauris, now an imprint of Bloomsbury Publishing Plc, 2006

Holland House: A History of London's Most Celebrated Salon. I. B. Tauris, an imprint of Bloomsbury Publishing, 2013

Talleyrand in London: The Master Diplomat's Last Mission. I.B. Tauris, an imprint of Bloomsbury Publishing, 2017

Anthologies, as editor:

Feasts (with Christopher Bland). Constable & Co., 1987
Proposals (with Laurence Kelly). Constable & Co., 1989
Happiness A Treasury (with John Train) Mount Street, 2007
Animals and Us (with John Train). M.T.Train/Scala, 2011
Garden Magic (with John Train). M.T.Train/Scala, 2013
Joy of the Seasons (with John Train). M.T.Train/Scala, 2014
Consolations. Starhaven, 2017; memorial edition, 2019

Catalogue, as editor & writer:

Alyson: A Painter's Journey. James Spooner, 2008

***